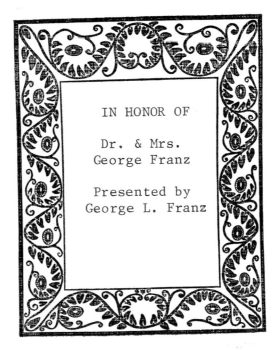

IN HONOR OF

Dr. & Mrs.
George Franz

Presented by
George L. Franz

FRANK CHAMBERLAIN PORTER

SOCIETY OF BIBLICAL LITERATURE
STUDIES IN AMERICAN BIBLICAL SCHOLARSHIP
SCHOOLS AND SCHOLARS

edited by

Robert W. Funk

and

E. Brooks Holifield

Studies in American Biblical Scholarship 1
Schools and Scholars 1

FRANK CHAMBERLAIN PORTER
Pioneer in American Biblical Interpretation

by

Roy A. Harrisville

SCHOLARS PRESS
Missoula, Montana

FRANK CHAMBERLAIN PORTER
Pioneer in American Biblical Interpretation

by

Roy A. Harrisville

Published by
SCHOLARS PRESS
for
The Society of Biblical Literature

Distributed by

SCHOLARS PRESS
University of Montana
Missoula, Montana 59801

FRANK CHAMBERLAIN PORTER

Pioneer in American Biblical Interpretation
by
Roy A. Harrisville

Library of Congress Cataloging in Publication Data
Harrisville, Roy A
   Frank C. Porter, pioneer in American Biblical
interpretation.

  (SBL studies in American Biblical scholarship ; 1)

  Bibliography: p.
  1. Porter, Frank Chamberlin, 1859-1946. I. Title.
II. Series: Society of Biblical Literature. SBL
studies in American Biblical scholarship ; 1.
BS501.P67H37   220.6'092'4   76-4498
ISBN 0-89130-104-6

Printed in the United States of America
Edwards Brothers, Inc.
Ann Arbor, Michigan 48104

PREFACE

The student of biblical studies, especially of New Testament studies in this country, has often suffered from an inverted hypocrisy, a disease which attained critical proportions during the Second World War. One symptom of the disease is the admission that biblical or New Testament research in this country has been a matter of little worth and that those who have pursued it belong to a genre far inferior to the continental. Who would dare compare the researches, say, of Henry Joel Cadbury on the Gospel of Luke with those of Adolf von Harnack, the studies of Kirsopp Lake on "family Theta" with the vastness of the enterprise of Constantine von Tischendorf, the Hellenistic and Philonic studies of a Frederick Clifton Grant or an Erwin Goodenough with the meticulous, bestially earnest work of an Erwin Rohde, an Eduard Reitzenstein or a Paul Wendland? How to counter the weight of a Lightfoot, a Westcott, a Hort or a Ramsey and all that noble company of Albion? For decades, American biblical students have been conditioned to expect something less from their countrymen, and as a result have ignored a century of their history. Those apt to teach or do research have read themselves myopic through the pages of an infinite number of strangers, some enjoying royalties through having interpreted the abstruse stuff, others through their mere translation.

The matter has been put testily, perhaps even Chauvinistically, and little is gained with trumpeting our discontinuity with Europe, as though mere immigration effected some radical transformation of the intellectual enterprise called the "humanities." We have had enough of that "myth" according to which any Natty Bumpo with a will can treat the world as his oyster.

Still, a man ought to know who he was before he dies.

Those years of scholarly activity in this country, extending roughly from 1890 to 1940, give identity to many of us responsible for biblical studies here. And, in many ways, those years were our better part — they marked an eminently fruitful period in American scholarship, and in the opinion of some, the most fruitful to date. Again, the span of years marked off by those dates is complete and ready to hand. What's done is done, and only a few whose activity fell in that period are still alive to tell. This guarantees a certain distance and dispassionate quality to that era's research, should anyone undertake it, though there is scarcely such a thing as "objectivity" without appetite.

The study of Frank Chamberlain Porter, teacher of the Niebuhrs, was an "accident." Responsible for a chapter on American lives of Jesus published in a volume dealing with the "New Quest," and afflicted with the aforementioned malady — indeed, by that time having become a "carrier" — I proceeded to reinforce my prejudice against the American sector of Jesus-research. The result was a pity, but as I then believed, happily corresponded with the bias. There was one exception — Benjamin Wisner Bacon, a prodigious and ingenious scholar whose capacity compelled his European counterparts, then as now, to pay him notice. Bacon, it appeared, was a fluke, a *Wunderkind* in midst of a race of pedestrian hacks. It was impossible not to be attracted to him. And, he made frequent reference to an old friend and Yale colleague, Frank Porter, whom he believed supplied that orientation of thought which his more erratic studies wanted. Bacon's work constituted a welter of books, monographs, essays and reviews, ranging from Saul the hashish eater through the Jewish lunar calendar to Jesus' secret anointing in the home of Simon the leper. But there was a coherence and consistency to Porter's less precipitous output which made his portrait a greater delight to draw.

Throughout the research, the conviction grew that Porter's conscious or unconscious urge to maintain continuity with English thought, which caused him drastically to revise a heritage of ideas as "native" as this country has yet produced, renders him a type of many of his contemporaries and successors.

Porter, as many of his kind, gave verbal instruction to his family to destroy his notes and correspondence when he died. Fortunately the request was not carried out. In addition to the seventy-odd pieces which came from his pen and were released for publication, almost two hundred files of unpublished material were available to this study. The greatest number contained jottings and notes from Porter's vast reading, enough to give one the suspicion that while Bacon wrote, Porter *read* books. The smaller number comprised Porter's unpublished manuscript, "The Religion of the Spirit," together with his lectures in Old and New Testament theology and their supplements. Until recently, all the unpublished materials remained in the old house on Bradley Street in New Haven, long since occupied by renters, the more recent of which turned that portion of the house where the files were kept into a rabbit hutch. The omnipresent offal, the pages chewed and shredded, the dust and stench — symbolic, perhaps, of the oblivion to which Porter has been consigned — force the reader to place merely provisional trust in the author's pagination of his unpublished works. In addition, thousands of Porter's notes made use of that "system of abbreviations," popularized by one Andrew J. Graham in 1857, and which Porter used for all his notes and lectures.[1] Taking in a sentence of Porter required mastery of his systematic though bizarre shorthand.

This volume opens with a biographical brief, touching only the barest essentials of Porter's life. The reason is not that his existence was a bland, dispirited thing. It had more than its share of adventure, even tragedy, enough to bring out a tough gentleness in the man once described as "trailing the beatitudes." But "Bampa" Porter's progeny prefers to keep that part of his story to itself — the dead belong to those who loved them most. The study then proceeds to a description of Porter's hermeneutic, and concludes with an attempt to set his thought in the context of the revision of his heritage from Jonathan Edwards.

Thanks are due to the American Association of Theological Schools for a scholarship which made this study a light financial burden, and to Mr. Raymond Morris, one-time student of Porter and Trowbridge Librarian emeritus of the Yale University Divinity School for valuable assistance, as well as for relaxing the rules so as to permit me temporarily to expropriate materials from the Porter bequest. I am indebted also to Professor John Hurd, grandson-in-law of Frank Porter, who aided in the Bradley Street house cleanup; to the Rev. Michael J. Lockerby who assisted with the footnotes, and to Seminarian Christine E. Miller for preparing the typescript.

Roy A. Harrisville
Luther Theological Seminary
St. Paul, Minnesota

---

1. Frank C. Porter, "A System of Abbreviations," *Yale Divinity Quarterly* II, 3, January 1906, pp. 96-106.

CHAPTER ONE

BIOGRAPHICAL BRIEF

Frank Chamberlain Porter, the second child and second son of William and Gertrude Ellen (Chapin) Porter, was born on January 5, 1859. His father, a native of Lee, Massachusetts, great-grandson of Jonathan Edwards and son of an able lawyer, was graduated from Williams College at age nineteen. On completion of his theological studies at Union Theological Seminary in New York, William, prostrated with hemorrhages so severe he was given only a few years to live, sailed for Florida, regained his health and in 1853 moved to Beloit, Wisconsin, a town founded by the New England Immigrating Company in 1837. Shortly after the founding of Beloit College, William was retained as Professor of Latin and continued to instruct advanced students until well into his eighty-sixth year. Overcome by furnace gas at the tender age of ninety-five, he recuperated and lived two more years, dying on October 28, 1917.

Frank Chamberlain was born in Beloit, enrolled at the Academy or "Prep" in 1874 and entered Beloit College in 1876. The faculty numbered eleven, and classes were held at "Middle College," its construction begun in 1847, it was alleged to be the oldest collegiate structure northwest of Chicago. Of the two curricula offered — the philosophical and the classical — Porter chose the latter. In an autobiographical statement, he wrote that, toward the end of his college career, he became acquainted with the work of Julius Wellhausen through the writings of W. Robertson Smith and owed much to the convincing exposition of the new approach to biblical studies through the articles of Henry Preserved Smith of Princeton.[1]

Graduating from Beloit College in 1880, Porter lived a year in Chicago with relatives while employed in McClurg's bookstore, and in 1881-1882 studied at Chicago Theological Seminary. Following that year and a second at Beloit where he received the M.A. degree — custom had it that the degree be awarded upon evidence of "good behavior" for three years following graduation plus the payment of a fee — Porter spent a year at the theological school in Hartford, Connecticut (1884-1885), where his older brother, William Jr., had made his home. At year's end, Porter entered the Divinity School of Yale University, its faculty distinguished by such worthies as Noah Porter, president of the Divinity School and son-in-law of Nathaniel Taylor; Timothy Dwight the younger, George Park Fisher and William Rainey Harper. Porter completed his undergraduate course at Yale in 1886, writing the required thesis on a history of the Synoptic Problem and delivering a graduating address on the "Via Media in Theology." He then reentered the Divinity School, this time to pursue studies leading to the doctorate. Completing his dissertation on the subject of Jewish belief in life after death,[2] Porter received his Ph.D. in 1889 and in autumn of the same year took up teaching duties at the Divinity School. The faculty voted the young professor an annual salary of $350.00, requesting that he lecture on history contemporaneous with the New Testament. After the resignation of John E. Russell, Professor of Biblical Theology, in May of 1889, the Yale faculty voted to recommend Porter's appointment as Instructor in Biblical Theology at an annual salary of $1000.00. That year Porter read Emil Schürer with graduate students and twice a week held a seminar on New Testament theology, concentrating on the studies of Johannes Weiss. In March of 1891, the faculty unanimously agreed to recommend to the Yale University Corporation Porter's appointment to the Winckley Professorship of Biblical Theology, a new chair, at a salary of $2500.00, with the understanding that the amount should be increased to professor's pay as soon and as rapidly as instructional funds warranted. In June of 1891 Porter was married to Delia Wood Lyman, daughter of Professor C. S. Lyman of Yale, and eventually came to reside at 266 Bradley Street, New Haven.

In the fall of 1891, Porter began lecturing on Old and New Testament theology and chaired a seminar on Judaism. Porter wrote that, when he began to teach, he found himself obliged to work from the period between the Testaments back into the Old and forward into the New, giving special attention to apocalyptic literature. His notion of the New Testament, he added, was the usual one — Paul was responsible for Christianity's departure from the religion of Jesus. But evidence for this, Porter added, he found "quite lacking."

During the summer semester of 1892, Porter visited several of the universities of Europe. In 1895 he was ordained and appointed Trowbridge librarian. In the spring and summer of 1908, he made another trip to Europe, sailing for Italy in February. He remained in Berlin throughout the summer, spent September in England, delivered an address at the Third International Congress of Comparative Religions in Oxford and resumed his work at Yale in the academic year 1908-1909.

In August of 1924, Porter had his first "sabbatical" in thirty-five years of teaching, and together with his wife sailed to China, lecturing in the Theological Seminary of Peking University as well as at Ching Hue College. From Peking, he left for India and Ceylon, visited Egypt, Palestine, Constantinople and Athens, sailed in August for Montreal and after a month in New Hampshire returned to Yale. When he retired in June 1927 faculty and students presented him with an arm chair, set him in it and carried him home to Bradley Street. Two years later, Porter made a third voyage to Europe. On June 17, 1931, Yale awarded him a second doctor's degree *honoris causa*, his first granted by Beloit College in 1897.

Delia Lyman Porter died in 1933, at the age of seventy-five years. Frank outlived his wife by thirteen years, dying on January 24, 1946, at the age of eighty-seven.[3]

---

1. Frank C. Porter, "Toward a Biblical Theology for the Present," *Contemporary American Theology*, Theological Autobiographies, ed. Virgilius Ferm, Second Series (New York: Round Table Press, 1933), p. 202.

2. Frank C. Porter, The Doctrine of Resurrection in Pre-Christian Judaism: Its Religion and Psychological Presuppositions, its Place in Jewish Thought, and the General Factors Determining its Development (unpublished Ph.D. Dissertation, the Divinity School, Yale University, 1889).

3. A letter of Lyman E. Porter, Frank Chamberlain's second son, dated May 23, 1967, indicates that the family is in possession of little information regarding Porter's early years. For such autobiographical information as is available, the reader is referred to "The Liberal and the Ritschlian Theology of Germany," *The Andover Review*, XIX, July 1893; "The Christian Way of Knowing, Thinking and Acting," Commencement Address, Yale Divinity School, June 1927, *Yale Divinity News*, November 1927; "Toward a Biblical Theology for the Present," *op. cit.*, as well as to Benjamin W. Bacon, "A Devoted Teacher," *Yale Divinity News*, May 1929, and Roland Bainton, *Yale and the Ministry* (New York: Harper and brothers, 1957).

CHAPTER TWO:

PRINCIPLES OF INTERPRETATION

I: *Historical Criticism*:

In contrast to many of his contemporaries, Porter was consistent and forthright in the enunciation of his presuppositions. First of all, he allowed the necessity of historical criticism, writing that Christian knowledge neither anticipates nor is suspicious of scientific labor, but adopts toward it a stance of "waiting and welcome."[1] Porter insisted that every clergyman, as the professional representative of the Christian religion in his community, should meet science's challenge by possessing at least the "safeguard" of a sound historical method and a trained historical sense.[2] For this reason, a knowledge of Greek was requisite to an understanding of the life and teachings of Jesus, and for special research into the background of Gospel history Hebrew was indispensable. Porter decried the "disastrous" divorce of the study of Christianity from the practical work of ministers and churches, contending that a "return to Christ" was precisely by way of historical study.[3] He contended that if theological seminaries abandoned the teaching of principles and method in favor of anticipating practical concerns, the seminary should be not simply reformed but abolished.

Something of an apologetic motif underlay Porter's insistence upon historical method. He believed that the way by which to avoid the "fatal danger" of allowing the educated classes to become irreligious or substitute philosophy for religion was to keep faith on its intellectual side within the sphere of contemporary knowledge, and cited Matthew Arnold to the effect that "what distinguishes culture . . . is that it is possessed by the scientific passion as well as by the passion of doing good."[4] Consequently, the historical or scientific study of religion must proceed, not merely for the sake of Christian believers, but for the sake of that increasing number "who will not see the truth of religion at all if it does not express its facts and claims in a language which they can understand."[5] Porter clearly admitted that the historical method necessitated a reconsideration and restatement of theological positions. He wrote of science's creating a new universe and of its forcing religion not only to change its formulae but to reconsider its grounds and defenses. But, he was confident that the distinction between things greater and less required by the historical study of the Bible was such as religious insight or religious experience would recognize.[6]

Though Porter regarded opposition to attempts to recover the historical Jesus on the part of continental theologians such as Martin Kähler of Halle, Germany, as tantamount to a rejection of the historical critical method,[7] he reserved his bitterest judgment for the "Princeton Theology." In a review of essays authored by the faculty of Princeton Theological Seminary in 1913, Porter conceded that the authors' discrediting of modern biblical criticism was no doubt undertaken in the interests of faith, but added that the sacrifice of faith in the human mind and its capacity to reach the truth for the sake of faith in Christianity was a "dangerous form of unbelief in God." Censuring the volume for its exclusivistic spirit, he denied that the doctrine of the essays was the teaching of Scripture and concluded by affirming the necessity of historical method and, in particular, the rediscovery of Jesus.[8]

Porter often referred to historical method as emancipating men from superstitions such as were reflected in the accounts of first and last things, the descriptions of heaven and Sheol, angels, demons and the like, and wrote that we need nothing but an historical explanation so as to be freed from further responsibility.[9] The emancipation from dogma, particularly the dogmatic use of the Bible, Porter viewed as twofold. First, critical method rendered Scripture kin to all other literature.[10] Second, such method freed men from the conventional assumption of the Bible's uniqueness and hence its authority to command conduct and belief. This assumption, said Porter, was reflected early in the life of the church, particularly in the canonization of the Gospels — a process which derived from the conviction that the time of God's immediate presence was past. The net result was to discourage the new prophet, to sacrifice freedom to the authority of a sacred text and to hinder progress in thought and morals. The early community could scarcely have done otherwise, in face of movements which threatened to sever its historical connections, but by constructing a canon the church acknowledged that it belonged to a decadent period and had no option but to worship the past.[11]

On the credit side of the ledger, Porter contended that historical method yielded a view of the Bible which reflected a great advance.[12] Armed with his critical tools, the student could note the development of Israel's religion from the idea of God as a tribal, national deity to the knowledge of Him as the only God of nature and mankind. He could trace the movement from nationalism toward universality, from ritual toward ethical religion, from legalism toward a religion of the Spirit. And since this advance derived less from some inner tendency than from the "constant and desperate struggle of the few," culminating in Jesus who effected that fusion of religion and morals which it was the glory of the prophets to have set on its way, the study of history yielded not only movements, but men as well.[13] It furnished an understanding of the great personalities of the Bible, and, above all, an understanding of the person of Jesus.[14]

The result, for Porter, was "a new Bible."[15] Between the extremes of viewing the Bible as a final record and interpretation of past fact and of holding it as outgrown and useless, three uses commended themselves to the modern man. The Bible could be used for the "large and varied humanity with language in it for all our higher moods"; for the "greatness of the human history of which it tells," or for guidance and inspiration "in our present search for God" according as the prophets, Jesus or Paul, appeared to furnish the truth best fitted for the time.[16] Again and again, Porter contended that such freedom as historical criticism guaranteed is consonant with the religion of Jesus who "did not intend to give us definiteness, but freedom," as well as with the religion of the New Testament which was "meant to give man freedom and not to bind him even to himself," thus enabling the whole man with all his human interests and deeper spiritual desires to make his way to the real heights of biblical literature and through those heights to the experience of God.[17] Porter wrote:

> Not piety in an age of liberty, but Christian liberty, the liberty which is piety, is what our age of intellectual liberty and of subjection to material power most needs.[18]

Porter was more specific about the achievements of historical criticism when it came to the question of miracle and, in this connection, struck his favorite theme, "the Religion of the Spirit." In contrast to an earlier age for which the place of the earth was central and the prevailing theory a kind of dualism, Porter characterized his own time as unable to believe in the intervention of supernatural powers and as regarding the position of our earth within the universe as insignificant.[19] Indeed, the word "miracle" constituted an offense to the modern mind.[20] The historical spirit, then, was calculated to lift us "out of regions where religion likes to stay," and to affirm strange events as merely problems to be solved, not as evidence of a second order of reality.[21]

Consonant with this view, Porter interpreted the visions and auditions of the Old Testament prophets in terms of mental experiences capable of psychological explanation, or referred them to emotional experiences which were seen in retrospect as having been a means by which truth was gained. Thus the vision of Isaiah occurred in a crisis of high emotion. It may have involved an actual loss of consciousness, but its significance lay not it its objectivity as vision, but in its taking place in the most inward and exalted regions of spiritual life. And it was not vision, but rather insight and moral judgment on which Jeremiah rested the most incredible of his forecasts — the overthrow of Jerusalem.[22] Porter contended that the older argument from prophecy which viewed each prediction as the occasion for a corresponding historical event had been displaced by the broad outlines of a religious development to which the great prophets furnished the stimulus.[23] As for Jesus, his consciousness of Messiahship did not derive from ecstatic emotion or objective vision. It was rather by way of sober judgment that he joined himself to John's movement, was baptized by him and came to a new self-awareness. The voice from heaven was thus a voice in Jesus' own soul.[24] Further, since Jesus did not perform miracles of healing as signs, his religion could not be seen to consist in any external or prodigious quality, but rather in a radical inwardness. His ministry of healing was thus subordinate to his ministry of the spirit and could thus be withdrawn from the category of miracles commonly defined. The true miracle, then, which it is the distinction of the Christian religion to affirm, is that of Jesus' character or personality and his influence.[25]

Porter entertained a like aversion to the apocalyptic element in the Bible. It was not ignorance, however, which lay at the heart of his distaste for it. As noted, his Ph.D. dissertation dealt with Jewish belief in life after death.[26] From a contemporary perspective, perhaps, the piece has more the aspect of a primer than a scientific study, but it was among the first of its kind. Porter knew enough about the subject, for example, to pen a classic review of George Foote Moore's *Judaism*. He reproached the Harvard scholar for confining his research to Haggadic materials, and thus for designating Judaism of the Tannaim as normative, and argued that apocalyptic and its historical occasions radically affected the religion of Judaism.[27] But he insisted that apocalyptic was not the whole of it and faulted Oxford's R. H. Charles for approaching Christianity exclusively along the line of apocalyptic and for assuming that the apocalyptic stream was wholly diverted from Judaism into Christianity.[28]

Porter described the accent on apocalyptic as a momentary fad of critical scholarship. He saw in it the lack of a strong ethical appeal, a lack which he assessed as a "fundamental mistake in Judaism."[29] For example, he noted what he called an "ethical decline" in the development of the idea of resurrection from the notion of it as occurring for the sake of the Jewish nation, through the idea of the individual's resurrection as coinciding with the nation's restoration to that of its displacing national revival. Judaism, said Porter, was not made better by this effort.[30] Like the older prophets, Jesus distanced himself from apocalyptic, but to the degree the prophets shared apocalyptic hopes in the nation's restoration, Jesus distanced himself from them as well.[31] There was then, an inherent inconsistency in prophetic preaching. It developed the concept of God toward monotheism, but never fully dissolved the connection which bound God to Israel. It "claimed all things for God," but did not "find God in all things, nor consecrate all things to God."[32] Thus, though the term "prophetic" characterized Jesus' ministry more than any other, to the extent the prophet still claimed the prerogative of a peculiar and exclusive love of God for Israel, signalled in the Messianic hope and thus in the outward and external, to that extent Jesus' career was discontinuous with prophetism.[33] For this reason, Porter's reflections on the question of Jesus' Messianic consciousness tended to negative results. He admitted that in his exposition of Jesus' teaching he put less and less stress on the Messiah-idea, for the reason that the more he studied the Jewish Messianic idea the less vital, direct and literal Jesus' connection with it appeared to be.[34]

Porter continued that because of Jesus' distance from apocalyptic, he could not have used the Son of Man title merely in self-designation, but rather applied it to all men. This did not deny eschatology to Jesus altogether — he did, after all, share the mood of his age — but for him the coming of God's Kingdom was not a phenomenon reserved for heaven or for Israel, but a power present here on earth. Jesus, then, did not postpone applying his principles to his own life.[35] How then explain the emergence of apocalyptic in the New Testament? Porter replied that the sayings of Jesus which in their best attested form and context are "paradoxical expressions of ethical truths" or combine the "highest, hardest ethical duty and the freest and most generous grace,"[36] were soon carried by early tradition into the area of eschatology. Thus, whether miracle or apocalyptic, everything was made to serve Porter's canon according to which the supernatural was to be sought within the natural and was not in any physical sense separate from it.[37]

If for Porter historical study spelled emancipation, he was not unaware of criticism's limitations. He stated that the facts about the Gospels which historical study can recover are "things" which in themselves do not give the knowledge of persons:

> Something more subtle and intangible than bare facts must constitute the essential quality of a book which contains the secret of a great personality and carries powerfully forward the influence of one who powerfully moved his fellowmen.[38]

Facts, then, are of a piece with the past, a return to which is inconsistent with the idea of development. They suggest an "abstract ideal,"[39] historical study yielding data accessible largely only to historians.[40] This last point was most significant for Porter, whose writings give ample evidence of his struggle to translate the results of theological scholarship for the "common reader." He wrote that "if historical research were the condition of a right religious use of the Bible, the book would be taken from the hands of the people."[41] In reference to the "return to Jesus," Porter affirmed that the Christ whom religious experience requires is one to whom historical study can bring us near, but insisted that even if historical science could get back to Jesus, such a return would satisfy only the intellectual sense. The way to Christianity was something more, and, in attempting to get at the historical Jesus, the scholar might even be on the wrong trail.[42] Thus, Porter agreed that there were parts and aspects of the Bible on whose "religious use" historical studies had no influence, portions such as could be enjoyed by children, or even by mature men and women, and in a fashion determined by something else than the reader's learning. And, while urging that the advantages of historical-critical method be made available to children, Porter cautioned the critic lest he spoil for them the charm of the biblical narratives, for, as he put it, the Bible has "religious power in itself apart from the historical facts and independent of their recovery."[43] The bondage, then, from which historical study sets us free, is never so great as to prevent spiritual profit and satisfaction in the reading of the book. The greatest books, he said, need such intervention of learning least.

Of greater significance to Porter, however, was the fact that an inevitable uncertainty attached to the results of critical research. In the matter of Gospel criticism, he contended that historical studies rendered certain data insecure. Faith, however, could not rest on the results of scholarly activity, no matter how total its impression, say, of the character or inner life of Jesus.[44] For this reason, faith required a certainty and a permanence rooted in experience which research either could not or was not concerned to yield. Porter wrote: "Not all those words of Jesus which the historian leaves unquestioned have equally the quality of universality and permanent validity."[45] No mere matter of fact per se, which it was the business of science to determine, could be made essential to religious faith. Consequently, faith should neither make affirmations of its own upon such matters of fact, nor be vitally dependent upon the affirmations of science. Indeed, religion might interpret facts and put them to "spiritual uses," but such interpretation should not be conditioned by the actuality of facts in nature or history which science must investigate and thus question or deny.[46] Faith, Porter concluded, must be liberated from dependence upon anything science shakes.[47] Finally, if for Porter the pursuit of scientific studies at the expense of the "higher uses and enjoyments" of literature was an ill, clearly the fundamental incapacity of historical research to provide an adequate basis for faith was a good. In regard to the "quest of the historical Jesus," he wrote:

> It may be that such disappointment as history has for us in our effort to get back to Jesus is for our good. If we could literally get

back to him, could we also spiritually move forward in him? Certainly we could do so only in some such way as the first Christians did, by some measure of disregard for what was past, by the possession of the Spirit of Christ as an indwelling, divine power.[48]

II. *The Appreciative Method:*

For Porter, then, historical criticism was not the "highest and fittest use" to which the Bible could be put. If language is not a perfect copy and embodiment of thought, but merely current coin for an exchange of thought which passes for more than its apparent value, an exchange dependent upon a background or basis of life and fact behind and beneath the words, then religion must "help science to see in men and movements the hand of God."[49] In concert with this insistence upon a supplement, Porter wrote that in respect of those who seek righteousness but are not at home in the churches, it would not do to adjust the Christian message to their point of view by avoiding all that would distinguish it from science, philosophy or sociology — it was rather "religion, the religion of Christ" which they required.[50]

Porter described the way in which this supplement was to be achieved in various ways. He wrote of getting into the "mental atmosphere" of an author, of changing one's presuppositions for his, or of being addressed as the author addressed his contemporaries.[51] He appealed for "insight" and "sympathy,"[52] "spiritual response," "tact,"[53] and "communion of soul."[54] Such "sympathetic insight," wrote Porter, was less a knowledge of things than of persons, and by a person. Repeating the question of Matthew Arnold — "Shall we enjoy the Bible?" — Porter spoke of the needed supplement as a "simpler and more direct use of the book as it is," an "emotional appreciation of its qualities," or a "more inward response to the spirit that moves in it."[55] Elsewhere, he stated that the task of making the past live again — the most religious use of a sacred literature — remained essentially the "work of imagination," a labor which must take precedence over historical research.[56]

Thus, while agreeing that no part of the Bible lies outside

the field of historical criticism, Porter advocated an appreciative beyond the merely historical or critical approach to the "real value of the Bible." He constantly reiterated his conviction that to unlock the secret of the Bible's religious power we must turn to its character as "literature." The "unembarrassed application" of the standards of literature to the more difficult portions of Holy Writ would save their beauty and their impressiveness for those unable to regard them as literal fact. It was just such an approach as was reflected, e.g., in the Oxford lectures of Bishop Robert Lowth, which reflected the oldest and most universal use of the Bible. Hence, after a "sane philosophy," the biblical student needed nothing so much as training in the principles and practice of literary criticism, in the nature of greatness in books, and in the application to the biblical materials of principles which condition the right reading of great books.[57]

Porter had little doubt regarding the species of literature to which the Bible belongs. It was, he insisted, chiefly "poetic" in character:

> The place of the sacred book in the Christian religion has been and must in the end be fixed by what can only be called, in the highest sense of that word, its poetic quality, by the universal truths which it so pictures that they are "carried alive into the heart by passion," not by the particular facts which it enables us to know.[58]

The greatest men in Israel's history were poets, wrote Porter, and it was poetry that described the unique relationship between Jahveh and his people.[59] He contended that in many parts of the Old Testament it is beyond dispute that the greater value lies in the poetic, on the "surface" rather than in the obscurities of tradition or historical fact beneath.[60] In regard to the New Testament, Porter described the elimination of the poetic for the sake of those "historical realities" which it had overlain as a sin equal to the confusion of poetry with prose or the elevation of prose to the level of a dogma. He asked:

> What if that which [the historian] clears away has the character not of intellectual theory but of poetic imagery . . . May it not then

prove to be true that in that which lies over the features of Christ in the New Testament, that in which historians have been inclined to see a veil that hides his face, we ought rather to behold the radiance that illumines it?[61]

For Porter, approaching the Bible from a "literary" point of view meant using it in the "poetic" sense. And because he believed the beauty of the biblical narratives to be a concomitant of their religious power, he could quote Keats' "Ode to a Grecian Urn" ("'beauty is truth, truth beauty,' — that is all ye know on earth, and all ye need to know") in support of his argument that "wherever heights of religion are reached, there is beauty."[62] No doubt, lest he be accused of substituting the dogmatism of a purely formal or aesthetic use of the Bible for that of canonicity or inerrancy, Porter added the qualification that it was perhaps more important to get at the "spirit of the poetry" than at the poetry itself.[63] And, of course, at the heart of Porter's advocacy of the appreciative or poetic approach, was his insistence that the Bible be intelligible to all and in their own tongue.

Consonant with his emphasis upon the poetic character of the Bible and the appreciative or literary approach to it, Porter turned to Aristotle, to the Greek rhetorician Longinus and to William Wordsworth. Early in his career, Porter wrote that in addition to Wordsworth's *Prefaces to the Lyrical Ballads*, he gleaned more help toward answering Arnold's question ("Shall we enjoy the Bible?") from Aristotle's *Poetics* than from the writings of theologians or historians. Noting that the *Poetics* were not much used by theologians, he urged that the Bible interpreter learn from the ancient Macedonian a love for melody and rhythm and extracted from the *Poetics* a principle he believed gave needed help toward solving the problem of the Bible's relevance, the principle that "truth is a higher thing than fact." In Aristotelian terms, poetry, and thus the Bible, expressed the universal element in human life. It disclosed the universal in the particular, and represented things as they *ought* to be, for "it is not the function of the poet to relate what has happened, but what might happen, what is probable or necessary." Wordsworth's "Michael" then served as a modern illustration of the old Aristotelian dictum.[64] Hence, though the poet's description of the universal might be a description of things as they are — viewing the universal in the concrete, or "imitating" the concrete in sense pictures — the poet still recreated those things by making the impress of the ideal upon them clearer than it is in nature. The poet was thus more concerned to relate things in an ideal order and unity, more concerned with observing the "law of inner poetic truth" than with relating events as they occurred or with observing the "law of outward physical nature." From this Porter concluded that unhistorical elements are not inconsistent with poetic truth, appealing to Homer "who knew how to make the impossible appear natural," and to Coleridge, whose plan for his *Lyrical Ballads* was to write poems in which the incidents and agents were to be in part supernatural, and cited Coleridge's "Rhyme of the Ancient Mariner" as an illustration of the poet's use of "probable impossibilities." This Aristotelian test of universality enabled one to draw the necessary distinction between things of lesser and greater value among biblical interpretations.[65]

To Longinus, the author of PERI HUPSOUS,[66] Porter again and again made reference when describing the stance or attitude which the interpreter must take toward the Bible. He wrote that it was hard to find a discussion of the doctrine of Scripture by a theologian which contained as much value for contemporary purposes as was offered by that ancient Greek rhetorician's treatise on great writing. Pleading Longinus' relevance to the specifically biblical interpretive task by stating that he dealt not merely with poetry but also with poetic prose, Porter, citing Prickard's translation (1906) and Saintbury's *Loci Critici* (1903), summarized Longinus' position as requiring "transport and wonder" for the reading of great books. According to Longinus, a book's authority is inward and its greatness to be found in its power, not its inerrancy. The secret of that power resides in the greatness of the writer's thought and intensity of feeling or in his own "greatness of nature."[67] Such "spiritual qualities" determine the choice and fit ordering of beautiful words and in a "mysterious way create in them a body in which the soul lives on and works effectively." Thus,

> the great book does not persuade but transports, does not inform but inspires. . . . Our proper response to the book is therefore exultation of spirit and quickening of thought, but at the same time wonder and awe as in the presence of the divine. . . . We are to go beyond the book by the impetus which the book itself gives, and are always to return to the book again for fresh impulse.[68]

In scores of ways, Porter reiterated the Longinian theme:

> The greatest products of the human spirit should be read with transport as if the words were our own, and with reverent wonder because of their divine excellence and power.[69]

There must be "wonder as well as information:"[70]

> We should read [the Bible] freely and reverently (with "transport and wonder") according to our inner need and response, for our spiritual good. . . . We should read it . . . to share the confidence and be stirred by the joy of the discoveries and creators of our higher life.[71]

The sequence transport *and* wonder was important to Porter. For him, "wonder" represented an attitude which could culminate in Christologies which remove Christ from the Christian and for which he nourished considerable distaste:

> It is wonder that makes of Christ a problem; and if we begin with wonder we are likely to end with the problem unsolved. But if wonder follows ecstasy, if reverence toward Christ results from the uplift that we receive from him, from our vision of his likeness to us and the impulse and power to be like him; then we know what it is that calls forth our wonder.[72]

If the poetry of Coleridge reflected one aspect of the Aristotelian theme, viz., that truth is higher than fact, and thus cast on the common and actual an unfamiliar and almost supernatural light, it was the poetry of Wordsworth which Porter believed most completely represented the ancient ideal. Wordsworth was that modern poet "most nearly prophetic" in his inspiration. Porter thus could illustrate the nature of the authority of Jesus' words as well

as the place of the Bible in the Christian religion by
comparing them with themes found in Wordsworth's "Ode
to Duty."[73] On numerous occasions, he would quote a
sentence from Wordsworth which he stated "has proved
more than anything else helpful in setting the mind forward
toward a view of scripture which satisfies both reason and
soul," and which for him best summarized the totality of the
ancient ideal:

> Aristotle, I have been told, has said that Poetry is the most
> philosophic of all writings: it is so; its object is truth, not individual
> and local, but general, and operative; not standing upon external
> testimony, but carried alive into the heart by passion; truth which
> is its own testimony, which gives competence and confidence to
> the tribunal to which it appeals, and receives them from the same
> tribunal.[74]

To that phrase, "carried alive into the heart by passion,"
Porter returned almost as often as to Longinus' call to
"transport and wonder." But in addition to deriving from
Wordsworth support for the inwardness of the Bible's
authority, Porter found the poet's "towering greatness" in
his power to find spiritual significance in common things. In
Coleridge's *Confessions of an Inquiring Spirit* or *Letters on
the Inspiration of the Scriptures* Porter detected a "certain
unadjusted dualism" between human and divine, but in
Wordsworth's "Resolutions," "Independence" or "The
Leech-Gatherer" he saw reflected an infinitely greater type of
poetry which gave the unfamiliar and unreal an almost
human aspect, or gave "the charm of novelty to things of
every day."[75]

"Truth is higher than fact"; great literature requires
reading with "transport and wonder," requires being
"carried alive into the heart by passion," gives the "charm of
novelty to things of every day" — such dicta for Porter all
described the horizon of the interpreter's task. Though he
stated that Arnold's insistence upon the absolute
subordination of the uses of historical method to the sphere
of conduct and the inner life suggested the substitution of a
new set of dogmas for old,[76] he nevertheless agreed that a
proper interpretation of, for example, the Gospels required a

"response to the personal presence of Jesus" who had become a "sort of conscience to every man."[77] "Sympathy," "fellow-feeling" and "a sense of wonder" were thus identified as those "moral qualities" which continually react upon critical study, and are superior to intellectual powers and training. Thus the least disinterested person, the "person most agreeing and most admiring," would give the truest exposition of Scripture.[78] The Christian, therefore, because of his "friendliness, respect, and good-will" toward Jesus, because of his "simplicity and sincerity . . . trust, humility and unselfishness" — living the life of Christ, enjoying a "spiritual likeness" to him, appropriating and repeating in his own experience "the things of the inner life" — was best able to understand him.[79] In support of his claim, Porter quoted the younger Dwight, who stated that, for an understanding of the Fourth Gospel, it was necessary to have "some comprehension of the inner life of a Christian believer who grows into the likeness of Christ by personal communion with Him."[80] Such a requirement, above all, was the experience of Jesus himself, as well as of Paul.

To the possible objection that his view of the Bible's authority as "inward," requiring to be read "according to our need and liking," or that his idea of religion, constituted as Coleridge's by "whatever finds me" in the Bible,[81] laid him open to the charge of subjectivism and modernizing, Porter gave ample reply. The orthodox, supernaturalist reaction stood in the way of a natural and rational reading of the Bible and hindered the application to it of the historical and literary methods which facilitate the understanding and enjoyment of other books. In particular, the orthodox view of Scripture had proved an obstacle toward finding the "Divine Spirit" in common as well as uncommon events, and above all in the sphere of the rational and ethical.[82] Porter could attack the dialectical theologians as advocating a like position, as eliminating from the Gospels everything moral and human.[83] But from whatever side the error, Porter stated that, when the object of study is the understanding of a person, distinctions between right and wrong historical procedures cannot be so easily defined, and one must have courage to assert that there is a subjective way toward reaching an objective goal. Such modernizing cannot be escaped and need not be feared. It is not only more important for the historian to be "courageously subjective" than to be in bondage to the word "scientific" — the more truly and deeply subjective he is, the better.[84] Hence, where recognition and response to the personal presence of Jesus in the Gospels is concerned, the perception of it, the value felt in it and the use made of it depends "more upon what one is than upon what one knows."[85] "Modernizing," for Porter, was thus a virtue and not a vice, provided it meant that "spiritual means can only be spiritually discerned."[86]

III: *The Result*:

Once Porter had applied his appreciative or literary method, miracle as prodigy and apocalyptic were virtually eliminated. It was the natural or common, first of all, not the supernatural, which was the truly moral. And since, as he believed, the laws of nature and the moral law were one and the same, the miraculous at least required definition in terms of God's activity within the course of nature, human history and the human mind.[87] And though Porter stated he would neither deny nor demand the miraculous for the sake of faith, he persistently sought the supernatural within the immanent.[88] The Bible itself, he contended, identified the natural, common, and ethical or moral, since of the various species of literature to which it could conceivably belong, that type which makes things reveal "unnoticed and rare beauties and truths" was its closest kin.[89]

As for apocalyptic or eschatology (Porter did not precisely distinguish the two), it too accented the outer, external and supernatural at the expense of the natural and common, and thus thwarted the essentially ethical character of the Christian religion. Indeed, apocalyptic originated in the transference of Jesus' "hard sayings" from the inner to the outer, from present to future, from earth to heaven.[90]

To the question, what remained of the biblical message once the supplement had been furnished, Porter responded: "The inner life of the divine and of man."[91] There first, "since if not there it makes little difference where else," we must seek and find God. The place of God's most immediate and demonstrable presence and work is thus our own "inner life" which, unlike the "outer," is of "essential and supreme worth."[92] With all their emphasis upon God's peculiar and special love for Israel, the great writing or pre-exilic prophets who comprised the center and soul of the Old Testament still proclaimed a Gospel of inwardness.[93] They were thus opposed to the priestly religion of rites. Amos, Hosea, Isaiah and Jeremiah all adopted the same negative attitude toward the cultus.[94] It was inwardness which preserved them from falling total prey to apocalyptic,[95] and in their higher moments rendered them critics of the national hope. Isaiah, for example, did not reinforce the popular belief that "God is with us." On the contrary, the destiny of the child prophesied in Isaiah 7:14, 8:8 and 9:3-7 contradicted the name "Immanuel," symbol of the people's spurious trust. And, Jeremiah saw Jahveh's true nature reflected not in the protection but rather in the destruction of the nation, and thus furnished stimulus for the revival and continuance of Jewish religion.[96] Ezekiel, of course, traduced that quality of inwardness by fortifying Israel's faith in God within the great walls of an isolating ritual.[97] The Deuteronomic, to say nothing of the Priestly Code with its attempt at combining the prophetic and priestly, conceded far too much to the external and outward, and hence reflected the same decline. Ritual and Torah were foisted upon the prophet, in whose place the scribe now appeared.[98] In all this period of decline, the wisdom literature constituted the grand exception. Unique, and in essence without Greek influence, it accented the inward and universal, thus marking the advance in spiritual religion.[99] To the extent of their emphasis upon the inner life and their opposition to ritualism and externalism, all these "radicals" of the Old Testament were a preparation for the ministry of Jesus.

For Porter, inwardness was the key by which to understand the religion of Jesus. Jesus' attitude toward the Old Testament, for example, was marked by freedom and inwardness. It was that of a normal attitude of mind toward a great literature.[100] Such inward appropriation or use of the Old Testament as determined by spiritual imagination and religious feeling Porter described as undermining the notion of a canon. Thus, as the prophets, Jesus opposed to the law of ritual or to a law constraining the will a law of the heart and unselfish ministry of love, an ideal of primacy through service and suffering.[101] Further, inwardness characterized Jesus' relation to prophecy. He "fulfilled" it to the extent he enjoyed that conscious and inward relation to it or sowed seed which germinated in other lives and grew to something greater than he imagined.[102] According to Porter, Jesus' parables reflected that inward quality to highest degree. The parables of the mustard seed and the leaven, for example, made clear that God accomplishes His purposes in an inward way, gradually and through ordinary forces and processes, not suddenly, violently, by intervening with power or creating something supernatural. Porter was sharply critical of Bultmann's interpretation of the parables as purely supernatural or eschatological.[103] For, he insisted, the difference between Jesus' religion and that of apostolic Christianity lay in Jesus' viewing every common thing in a divine light, not in beholding one great divine thing in a human aspect, accessible and loved.[104] Jesus thus almost always used the parables in keeping with Adolf Jülicher's definition, that is, in simple, homely and every-day fashion, and as requiring no interpretation. The reason for this was that Jesus knew God immediately from nature. Though Porter acknowledged this aspect to be subordinate, he still contended for its importance, no doubt because of its contrast to the prodigious and miraculous. At any rate, this ability to see God where other men did not furnished one reason why the disciples saw God in Jesus.[105]

Porter wrote that those difficult passages in Matthew 11:12 ("from the days of John the Baptist until now the kingdom of heaven has suffered violence, and men of violence take it by force") and Luke 17:20-21 ("'the kingdom of God is not coming with signs to be observed; nor will they say, 'Lo, here it is!' or 'There!' for behold, the kingdom of God is in the midst of you'") required interpreting in the same fashion — the Kingdom lay in the natural and common, a Kingdom to be found within oneself.[106] Even Jesus' death coincided with his description of the essence of religion as inward, as well as with his refusal to accept the prodigious as superior to the moral or ethical. It would have been unnatural, said Porter, for Jesus to accept on the simple authority of Scripture such a task which was not his own free choice, a task of which he was not inwardly convinced that it was God's will. Thus, Porter opposed to theories of vicarious and substitutionary atonement the idea of the believer's inward and ethical appropriation of Jesus' death, the will to make that death his own in character and conduct. Not a doctrine about the death of Christ, Porter wrote, but rather a dying to sin which is the moral task of all men was the greater thing.[107]

Nowhere were the results of Porter's use of appreciative method more transparent than in his exposition of the epistles and theology of Paul. At the outset, Porter averred that Paul had preserved most accurately the earliest conception of Jesus, that he had furnished the primary witness to Jesus and thus yielded the basis for a judgment of comparison between Judaism and Christianity. Agreeing that much came to Paul from the character of Christians who preceded him, Porter nonetheless insisted that the apostle was a witness to the actuality of Jesus' earthly life.[108] The Yale scholar was aware that these statements ran counter to the arguments of such as William Wrede, but to the latter's assertion that Paul had disregarded the historical Jesus for the supernatural Messiah, he replied that the Christ of Paul was not a mythological figure and that Paul knew the mind of Jesus as scarcely any other.[109] Porter spoke of the hymn to love in I Corinthians 13 as constituting an actual character-sketch of the earthly Jesus, a sketch which he regarded as entirely inexplicable apart from Paul's knowledge of the historical Jesus.[110] He likewise referred to Paul's use of the term "Abba" as convincing proof of the apostle's knowledge, and, most of all, contended that the agency of the historical Jesus marked what was distinctive in the apostle's concept of "Spirit." That is, Paul's notion of a second, "present coming" of Christ as Spirit, in addition to his historical appearance, was due to the strength and consistency with which he executed his portrait of the historical Jesus.[111]

Critical of all nineteenth century quests for the historical Jesus which were unable to unite all the conditions for a "true return" in a single experience, and out of sorts with the attempt of Wobbermin of Breslau to combine the concerns of Kähler, Herrmann and others by way of reducing the historical facts to the "personal life of Jesus," Porter contended that the views reflected in the varying and diverse quests could be united since Paul himself had achieved their union.[112]

Porter stated that the way by which the apostle reconciled the divine to the earthly Jesus was to apply two "tests" to all Christian thought. First, Christian thinking must be according to the historical Jesus, and second, it must be "natural" or true to one who has the "mind" of Jesus.[113] Porter gave maximum attention to the second of these two criteria. In *The Mind of Christ in Paul* he wrote:

> It is about the meaning of the love of Christ, and what it is natural for one who is constrained by that love to think . . . that we can learn . . . from the thinking of Paul. . . . Christian thinking then is not thinking about Christ, but thinking about other persons and things in the light of the knowledge of Christ.[114]

Porter contended that of all the ways in which men have tried to escape the difficult demands of Christ and Paul, the most dangerous have been those Christologies which are called high because of the distance by which they separate Christ from men. Whereas Christologies assume that Christ is a problem needing something else for its solution, to Paul the knowledge of Christ is the Christian's most certain possession.[115] Porter attempted to glean support for his contention in the suggestion that the apostle cannot be referred to as the author or advocate of such lofty Christological expressions as are found in the New Testament. Given the "tests" or criteria, Paul's method was to carry back the Christological categories he had inherited to the historical Jesus, conforming them to his character.[116]

The result, Porter wrote, was that however exalted and divine the nature and office of Christ may appear, they do not so transfer him to the side of God that he ceases to be a type of true humanity. Paul thus set aside such names or definitions of Christ's place and nature as threatened to displace him or separate him from men, or, he interpreted them for Christians, verifying them in the Christian experience.[117]

Porter argued that only two passages in Paul's letters appeared to offend against the apostle's tests — I Corinthians 8:6 and Colossians 1:15-17. Describing the text in I Corinthians as the first and "strange" appearance of a Logos Christology in Christian history, Porter maintained that Paul was not its author. He went on to state that Paul did not deny the truth of the creed, though he had nothing to say about what the creed affirms, since he merely alluded to it and did not care for it. Paul's instinct and inner preference was for the great Hebrew confession of God, the Shema, and his concern was for the love of Christ in the Christian, not with Christ's part in the universe. That is, at the point where we would scarcely expect to find the apostle proceeding according to his "tests," he applied the principle that thinking about Christ must be according to the Christian.[118]

Porter referred to Colossians 1:15-17 as standing in the strangest isolation. Refusing to eliminate the verses, he nevertheless argued that Paul was quoting a current Logos hymn to Christ which was not his own. Paul could affirm the words of the hymn, but he was more interested in Christ's place in the church than in the universe, in his making peace than in his making all things. Or again, in harmony with what he conceived Paul's criteria to be, Porter wrote that it is in the region in which the love of Christ operates that Paul ascribed to Christ the possession of all things, and consequently did not find it absurd to ascribe all things in like manner to the Christian.[119]

Porter wrote in essentially the same fashion of the hymn in Philippians 2:6-11. Here, he maintained, Paul also quoted a hymn he did not write, and by subjecting the hymn to Jesus himself changed it from its original purpose and employed it as "neither myth nor theology," but as a hymn to Jesus Christ, and in his image a hymn to self-sacrificing love. Porter stated that the idea of pre-existence implicit in the hymn was not to be viewed in Greek but rather in Hebraic terms, God having thought of or having planned for Jesus from the beginning of the world. Denying to Paul authorship of the Logos Christology in the passages cited, Porter summed up his position by writing that Paul had many Christologies, but that in each case he sought to subject the idea or concept to the character of the historical Jesus as well as to the Christian experience.[120]

For Porter, whatever of residue in Paul remained after his tests had been applied was to be construed after the rule of the relation between "reality and form." Since the language of Paul concerning Jesus is neither the language of doubt and fear, nor of intellectual curiosity and speculation, but rather the "language of emotion," and since for the right reading of a poet the question is irrelevant whether or not he supposes the concrete objects in which he clothes his thought and emotion are actual, whatever could not be subsumed under the Pauline "tests" Porter regarded as poetry.[121]

With reference to the Pauline phrase "in Christ," Porter contended that Paul, not only in what he said but in his life as well, told of Jesus; that the "new religion" was the religion of Christ in those in whom he dwells and that Paul's Christianity consisted in his inner experience that the "nature" of Christ has in it the power to recreate itself in other lives not his own. He wrote that in most expositions of Paul's Christianity more emphasis had been put upon his worship of Christ as divine, upon his belief in the death of Christ as a wholly unique redemptive work, as an atonement, a "wonder-working power," than upon his more emphatic and original, even astonishing assertion of the ethical — the oneness of Christians with Christ in all things. Porter constantly warned his readers against allowing Paul's "wonder" before Christ to obscure his sense of oneness with him.[122]

In his exposition of the idea of oneness, Porter first of all denied that it could be conceived in substantialist fashion.

He stated that Paul's mysticism was not substantialist, and that it was a mistake to construe the phrase "in Christ" as of physical substance. He rejected the notion that the preposition "in" had the power to bring in the whole substantialist schema and impose it upon the person of Jesus, and all because of his conviction that "substance is not greater but less than personality." Porter explained what he meant by stating that such "bald" expressions in Paul as "'Christ in me' need not be accounted for by viewing Jesus as changed from a historical person into an all-penetrating ether, refined but yet material." Or again, and in more graphic fashion, he wrote that "the oneness of the Christian with Christ is not in any sense, however refined, a mixture of two gases or fluids." Porter's foil, of course, was Adolf Deissmann, who appeared to construe existence "in Christ" in a sense analogous to that in which we are in an atmosphere or ether. And, Porter added, what constituted the chief difference between his and Albert Schweitzer's understanding of Paul was that, whereas Schweitzer interpreted Paul to say that one must first become supernatural in a physical, corporeal sense before he can receive the love of Christ, he, Porter, viewed Paul as regarding the man with Christ's love within him as a "supernatural being." Paul's view, then, did not result in a deification of man. Consequently, Porter denied that Paul conceived a mystical union with Christ — language which Porter stated was not Paul's own but that of his readers — in the Eucharist, in a doctrine of the Real Presence or in the fellowship of believers.[123]

Positively, Porter defined Paul's mysticism as "personal" or "spiritual." He could use traditional, biblical terms to define that personal, spiritual oneness, and could speak of Paul's experience of Jesus as "constituting his new self," an experience which constituted "Paul's Christian religion." He could also state that just as the self-emptying of Christ issued in God's raising him to a place of power and glory, so the Christian rises to a place of authority with him, adding that the consciousness of this oneness with Christ endangers humility, a peril to which the apostle was not insensitive, especially when forced to affirm the sincerity of his own unselfishness. It is Paul again, said Porter, who helps us determine the natural self-consciousness and self-assertion of complete love. And Porter could also write that the only difference between the resurrection of Christ and the believer's is that his was first, since prior to the death and resurrection of which Paul speaks in I Corinthians, there must occur that dying and rising again which are the condition of a man's belonging to Christ. A propos of this idea, Porter stated that we should not expect the Christian to be like Christ in the things that evidently set Christ apart, but that in fact the boldness of Paul's thought led him to affirm a oneness with Christ in precisely such things. Clearly, for Porter, "oneness" consisted in a "oneness of love." "If," he wrote, "there is a secret or mystery in Paul's phrase 'in Christ Jesus,' its solution is surely to be found in the nature of love." Or again, he spoke of "sharing the inner life of Jesus" in terms of the "contact of friendship with Christ," and made appeal to Benjamin Jowett, "that brilliant representative of a modern Paulinism," who drew the same conclusion. Porter also used the term "ethical" or "moral" to describe Paul's view of the believer's union with Christ, for if "substance is not greater but less than personality," for Paul, in contrast to the common understanding of life in the Spirit as a life characterized by supernatural powers and ecstatic experiences, "the highest supernatural is the highest ethical."[124] Porter asked:

> Are we to suppose that Paul thought of Christ as the Son in some sublime yet literal sense, through some substantial process by which God produced him, and because of which he shares what we can only express by calling it the *physical* nature of divinity; while upon us Christ confers sonship only in a purely personal, spiritual sense, only in the sense of love? If so, then Paul fell into our easy error of making the sonship of Jesus lower than our own by trying to make it higher.[125]

Since Jesus himself had repelled all worship of himself, or had no notion he was to stand between God and man, spanning the distance and overcoming that disposition in God which kept man estranged, speculation concerning

Jesus' metaphysical nature constituted an actual decline or barrier which Porter assigned to the "mighty spirit of the apostolic age." In reality, Jesus' sonship with God was typical and for the sake of the sonship of men.[126]

Paul's "hard sayings," i.e. those in which he identified the Christian with Christ's suffering, death, resurrection and glory, were to be interpreted in terms of love, friendship and morality. Thus, for Porter, the second of the Pauline criteria, viz., that Christian thinking should be natural to one who has the mind of Christ, was identical with the ethical or moral. When, for example, Jesus asserted his oneness with the Father, he meant something which belonged to human nature and not merely to himself. Jesus' approach to God was thus an approach open to man as man, by way of mysticism, goodness and beauty. Of the two "religions," the two "Christianities" in the New Testament — the metaphysical and the inward, moral, spiritual — that was newer, stranger and greater, contended Porter, which was revealed and created as God's gift to men.[127] When Paul could find the spiritual, personal or ethical in such formulations as I Corinthians 8 or Colossians 1, he allowed such Christological utterances to stand.[128]

As to the shape this oneness takes, Porter wrote that the one principle sufficient to guide us safely is Paul's own word, "be imitators of me, as I am of Christ." Paul's so-called mysticism was wholly controlled by his conception of the personality of the historical Jesus, oneness with whom meant imitating him, or as Porter put it, "taking upon oneself the task of Christ," "taking the place of Christ."[129] This personal, spiritual, ethical or moral oneness, said Porter, is not something of which the Christian is already in possession — it is an "ideal," for, as he wrote:

> Paul describes not a oneness with Christ that has been divinely given . . . but a oneness which is still before him as an ideal, a goal not yet attained but always the object of eager and anxious pursuit.[130]

To the possible objection that Paul had trajected his Gospel back into the life of the historical Jesus, Porter replied that the apostle may indeed have done so.[131] Paul, wrote Porter, was not bound to quote the words or imitate the outward ministry of Jesus. Indeed, by consciously and purposely departing from Jesus' example he remained truer to his spirit and purpose. This did not involve a deviation, however, but was in accord with Paul's intent to interpret everything by the historical Jesus.[132] On the other hand, Paul's standpoint regarding the law would have been inexplicable unless Jesus himself had not been directly opposed to it. Both the historical Jesus and Paul agreed in their rejection of an understanding of the Old Testament religion which the word "Torah" implied. Naturally, so as to justify his disregard of law, Paul required the ingenious doctrine of the cross which Porter reckoned as unconvincing. In the main, however, the various doctrines of Christ's death were "controlled" by the idea of Christ as the manifestation of love together with the requisite death and rising of the believer.[133]

Porter freely admitted that he derived the stimulus for his view of the Pauline "mysticism" from Jonathan Edwards. He stated that he did not know where to find a clearer recognition of that primary element in Paul's conception of Christ and the Christian than in Edwards' posthumously published "Treatise on Grace," and summarized Edwards' conception of the Christian religion as the entrance of the Divine Love into human beings and making them his own.[134]

When Porter came to summarize the thought of Paul, he spoke of him as the "great prophet of the Spirit," as developing a view of which the Old Testament had made but a beginning. The question confronting the apostle was: what should take the place of Jesus' presence after his departure from the earth? The answer, wrote Porter, lay in his concept of Spirit. It was "Spirit" which effected the adjustment between Paul's affirmation of Christ's pre-existence in the Logos Christology and his emphasis upon the resurrection in the "enthronement Christology."

The advantage of the term "Spirit," said Porter, is that it suggests both the divine energy from without as well as the voluntary movements of the inmost self and thus solves the problem of the relation between the external and inward, between the revelation of Jesus as objective but also inwardly experienced, or, between the ideas of gift and duty.

When Porter wished to detach the term "Spirit" from a dogma for the purpose of describing an experience open to every Christian, he used the term "immanence," though that term was not a favorite with him. Accenting Paul's interpretation of Jesus as "Spirit," Porter argued that if he were really the divine Reason, Word and Wisdom, men need not at all have known him as Jesus in order to know him as the eternal Christ. At the same time, he emphasized the historical Jesus as fundamental to the apostle's Christianity, concluding that Paul had developed his idea under the impulse and in the light which proceeded from Jesus' earthly life and character. Thus, the apostle's task of showing that Jesus' religion is inclusive of all true religion everywhere did not establish a new line but was in the line of Jesus himself.

For Porter, then, the "return" to the religion of, and the "return" to the religion about Jesus were one and the same. Conceding that the interpretation of Jesus by "Spirit" and the interpretation of "Spirit" by Jesus might tend in different directions — the one detaching faith from dependence upon the historical Jesus and the other accenting the historical Jesus as the abiding foundation of Christian faith — Porter contended that Paul had achieved the union of these and thus fulfilled the criteria or tests of a true "return."[135]

When Porter came to distinguish the Pauline letters from the synoptic Gospels, he reached again for Longinus' contrast between transport and wonder.[136] The Gospels, yielding the spirit and personality of Jesus, fell under the rubric of transport and constituted a necessary guide alongside the epistles.[137] And although he regarded the nature of our knowledge of Jesus gleaned from the Gospels as partial and imperfect, Porter viewed this as an advantage, as freeing us from the constraint of a literal commitment to the past and enabling us to appropriate Christianity as a religion of the Spirit,[138] or as evoking wonder at the sight of the divine beauty and excellence of Jesus' character reflected in the epistles. For this reason, Porter gave first place to wonder, since it guaranteed the knowledge of Jesus' spirit which criticism could neither sway nor deny.[139] As he put it, "if the Gospels furnish the facts, it is still Paul who provides the key."[140]

Of the Fourth Gospel, Porter wrote that it is quite incredible it could have been written without Paul, since a theological if not a literary relationship existed between them. In both the religion of Jesus is grasped as the religion of the Spirit.[141] Indeed, Porter continued, the purpose of the Fourth Gospel was to furnish the Christology of Paul a firmer foundation by making Jesus himself its advocate.[142] The situation, of course, had changed since Paul's time, and a transition was needed from the faith which first took shape against the law to a faith which took shape against a false wisdom.[143] In other words, the time had come when Paul's way was either too easy or too hard, and faith required a return to the actuality of the earthly life of Jesus.[144] Porter referred to the unhistorical procedure involved in the Fourth Evangelist's attempt to carry back into Jesus' earthly life all that the Spirit of Christ might teach and regarded the Gospel's accent on freedom as attenuated by its emphasis upon the finality of the revelation of God in the earthly life of Jesus. But, at the same time, he interpreted the Gospel's exclusivistic claim on Jesus' behalf in terms of its ascribing a real though unconscious Christianity to all who love.[145] Thus, the Gospel's greatness lay in its vindication of the right of every man and every age to find the divine and eternal in Jesus, a right affirmed by the promise of the Spirit who would take Christ's place and lead all men into truth.[146] And since, as he saw it, John's idea of the spiritual presence, viewed as the returning Jesus or as his spiritual "substitute," makes up the Gospel's chief thought, it assumes its proper place as the successor to the Pauline thought.[147]

Thus, over the distillate of his use of appreciative method, Porter could write one word — "Spirit." It was Spirit which characterized the inward and moral, Spirit marked the ultimate mediation between God and man, Spirit denoted the power of God manifest in human life and pointed to that "other way" left open in face of men's inability to resort to miracle as evidence of God.[148] Porter agreed that it was easier to use the term "Spirit" of whatever is inexplicable and mysterious in the realm of sense, for which reason it might appear ill suited to assist modern theology toward definiteness and clarity. But it was a term Porter could not spare. He chose it because he believed its Hebrew antecedents rendered it harmonious with his own emphasis upon the personal, the "spiritual" thus occurring not at the end of the natural, but at the end of the supernatural line of its development.[149] Porter qualified his position by stating that it was not the Hebrew conception of Spirit as such, viz., an exceptional force effecting occasional wonders in nature and human experience,[150] which was of value to modern theology, but rather an interpretation of it as the universal indwelling of God in nature, morals and in the man standing highest in that realm, the "genius."[151] To the "religion of authority" Porter thus opposed the "religion of the Spirit," a religion not submitted to in outward fashion, but inwardly experienced. Further, that term "Spirit" could also denote what is unlimited or universal. Still, Porter did not object to using the term "supernatural" if it marked the "realization of the highest ideal of character." He contended that Christianity's emphasis upon regeneration as divine deed, upon forgiveness and the gift of the Spirit tended to give persistence to superstition, adding that Christianity was often content to define the goal and duty of the Christian life in more or less external fashion. But he could retain the word "supernatural" in opposition to, for example, the Unitarians, whose translation of Christianity into merely rational terms rendered it easy of acceptance.[152] Porter nevertheless emphasized that the term "Spirit" had the advantage over the term "supernatural," inasmuch as it inclined toward the inner and easily made way for the ethical by the side of or in the place of the miraculous. In support of his choice, Porter appealed to a "typical modern theologian," Auguste Sabatier, and to a "typical modern philosopher," Rudolf Eucken. The former, he said, rejected authority in religion as outmoded and seized upon the word "spirit" to name the religion that is free. The latter rejected the current "monism" because of its tendency to materialism and found the term "spirit" conducive to a "higher realm."[153]

IV: *The Synthesis*:

Porter was not content with urging an appreciative approach to the Bible as a supplement to historical method. He sought more precise definition of the adjustment between the two concerns[154] and believed the problem was best illustrated by the relation between the "religious" and "historical" uses of the Bible, or between "historic fact" and "poetic truth."[155] The question of the relation between the historical Jesus and the Christ of faith was merely a "peculiar and difficult example" of the larger problem, analogous to that of the relation between the outward object and inner feeling in a work of art.[156]

Early on, Porter named three possible ways in which that adjustment or synthesis could be achieved. According to the first, each approach would have its own share of the biblical materials, leaving untouched what belonged to the other's sphere. According to the second, each would deal with the same materials, but enjoy independence as to methods and results. The third way Porter described as one of "interaction," not merely in fact but "by right."[157] Let science give aid to the religious experience which could proceed more safely and penetrate more deeply "on the ground of truth" than on the ground of error.[158] Then, let historical study by virtue of its inconclusiveness leave room or prepare for the religious use of the Bible. Early in his career, Porter discussed the "peculiar and difficult example" of the problem of relating science to faith and suggested a combination of these two concerns. He wrote that the antagonism between the two resolved into the question:

> Can the eternal, divine Spirit of Christ be best found and most surely and purely possessed by investigating and contemplating the man Jesus, of whom the gospels contain memories and impressions; or by observing how, especially in the first age, and there in original and normative fashion, the personality of the historical man of Nazareth became an inspiring, purifying, transforming power in the lives of his followers?[159]

Porter judged that the Ritschlian, in his insistence on the historical Christ as the ultimate revelation, ran the risk of contending "the better the historian, the better the Christian," a danger which could be escaped only by holding that the reality of this one fact must not be determined by historical evidence. The liberal, on the other hand, who found the ultimate revelation and authority in reason and conscience, was in danger of contending "the better philosopher, the better Christian." Both, Porter argued, avoided making the living Christ essential to faith, since the one held merely to the Christ of history and the other merely to the Christ-idea.[160] Porter concluded that the two "ways" need not be mutually exclusive in this country where the controversy had not yet divided modern theologians into warring camps and suggested that the "average man" should follow the leading of both schools, should "dwell with the man, Jesus of Nazareth, and learn to know God in the man," or return to the "Spirit of Christ" in Paul and the Gospels.[161] Subsequently, Porter clearly subordinated the concerns of history to those of faith, a theme struck earlier but not developed.[162] In this later period, Porter flatly stated that historical study was clearly subservient to the religious uses of the Bible and made renewed appeal to Aristotle, but especially to the German thinker Rudolf Herrmann Lotze — in particular, to one sentence in Lotze's *Microcosmos* which he described as "nothing less than a proclamation of emancipation."[163] Referring to Lotze's description of the long dispute between men's spiritual needs and the work of science, Porter quoted Lotze to the effect that each has its own right and that the mediation between them is to be found

> not in admitting now a fragment of one view and now a fragment
> of the other, but in showing how absolutely universal is the extent
> and at the same time how completely subordinate the significance
> of the mission which mechanism has to fulfill in the structure of
> the world.[164]

Porter stated that when he applied Lotze's rule to the Bible, he found that it yielded science an absolutely unrestricted freedom and yet allowed the worth of the book to the spiritual nature of man to remain unimpaired and supreme. "Just how this was to be," Porter confessed, "did not then appear; nor does it now always clearly appear. Yet I have found Lotze's words a good working hypothesis."[165] When the way by which the rule was to be applied did clearly appear to Porter, it was a "true life" or "faith" — "more eager to see God clearly somewhere than dimly everywhere" — which solved the problem of the relation between the historical and religious uses of the Bible and constituted that final step from historical probability to religious certainty.[166] In respect of the Old Testament, this meant that the question whether or not the history which science uncovers is unique (uniqueness denoting the special presence of God and of the other world) depends upon religious faith.[167] In terms of the "quest of the historical Jesus," it meant that whereas theology as the "science of religion" could only describe the actual place which Jesus holds in Christian faith or the influence which he exerts over human lives, religion or faith does not rest on the outward facts of Jesus' life but upon "something inward and spiritual" — his personality, his inner life, his character and influence. The place of the New Testament in the Christian religion is thus determined by the way in which it imparts the impression of Jesus' "personality."[168] Moreover, that which reaches a high plane of religious value or significance for the religious life reaches an equally high plane of probability as fact.[169] For example, Porter stated, the study of the Old Testament as religious literature leads to the same exaltation of prophecy to which we are led by using it as a collection of historical sources.[170] So the religious value of a historical record is itself a fact with which the historian must reckon. The value or power which the record possesses and which is due to the power the facts once had over the biblical author, may be valid evidence of the actuality of the events. Thus, Porter concluded, it is better to see the facts as the prophets and apostles saw them, "transfigured by faith and vitalized by passion," than to see them just as they occurred, for it is to that transfiguration that the facts owe their value and power.[171]

In another connection, Porter could describe the adjustment in terms of the relation between "form and spirit," with emphasis upon the latter:

> I think the way toward a right view lies along the line of the development of the *historical sense* in the child. . . . One who has something of the historical sense will not ask in regard to the stories of the early chapters of Genesis whether they are "fact or fiction," "the Word of God or mere human tradition." He will indeed attempt a distinction, but it will be the distinction between *form* and *spirit*, or letter and thought . . . [These stories'] value has always lain to the religious man and still lies to the scientific historian wholly and solely in the religious ideas they incorporate.[172]

For Porter, however, a "chasm" still yawned between faith and science. In terms of the relation between the historical Jesus and the Christ of faith, he described the problem as follows:

> We *think* that the total impression of the gospels gives a true image of the actual life and mind of Jesus of Nazareth; but . . . we *know* . . . that this impression is the image of ideal and perfected humanity. We *think* it to be historical fact; we *know* it to be universal truth.[173]

Porter preferred not to ground the thinking upon the knowing, but the other way around. He believed the total impression of the Gospels to be true because of the historical evidence they contain:

> I may say as a historical judgment, that it is difficult — it is in fact for me impossible — to account for the ideal and its effect without accepting the reality of the one who was great enough to reach the ideal in thought and life and so to express it in conduct and in word that it became a living power among men.[174]

At the same time, Porter acknowledged that such a conviction was a mere historical judgment; that, while Christian experience must remain a direct reproduction of the experience of the disciples, it could only be an indirect reproduction of the experience of Jesus. Ultimately, however, the "actuality" of Jesus, in contrast to his "picture" or "impression" ("unquestionably indispensable"), was expendable. In terms of that broader question of the relation between fact and poetic truth, Porter cited Bacon, Lord Verulam, to the effect that poesy

> was ever thought to have some participation of divineness, because it doth raise and erect the mind by submitting the shows of things to the desires of the mind, whereas reason doth buckle and bow the mind into the nature of things.[175]

In short, the question of the relation between the "actual" and the "impression" was one which left both poet and prophet "undisturbed."

1. "The Christian Way of Knowing, Thinking, and Acting," *op. cit.*, p. 6f.
2. "Peking Address," unpublished (1924); "Ought a Minister to Know Hebrew?" *The Congregationalist* (May 4, 1899), p. 633.
3. "The Ideals of Seminaries and the Needs of the Churches," *Yale Divinity Quarterly*, III (March 1900), p. 29.
4. "The Intellectual Value of Theological Training," unpublished (n.d.), p. 13.
5. "Some Recent Critical Studies in the Life of Christ," unpublished (1902), p. 1.
6. From an untitled piece on things greater and less in the New Testament, unpublished (n.d.), p. 16.
7. "The Higher Criticism and the Teaching of the Young," *The Bible and the Child*, ed. F. W. Farrar (New York: Macmillan and Co., 1896), p. 140f., and *New Testament Theology: Supplementary Material*, unpublished (1923-1924), p. 5.
8. "Princeton Theology," *Yale Divinity Quarterly*, IX (March, 1913), pp. 131-34.
9. "The Bearing of Historical Studies on the Religious Use of the Bible," *Harvard Theological Review*, II (July, 1909), p. 256.
10. An untitled fragment on the Spirit, unpublished (n.d.), p. 9.
11. An untitled piece on the relation of the New Testament to Jesus, unpublished (n.d.), pp. 4, 7, 11, 13, 15f., 20, 22f.
12. *Ibid.*, p. 23; Shorthand review of Theodore Munger's biography of Horace Bushnell, unpublished (n.d.), p. 1.
13. "Historical Facts and Religious Values in the Old Testament," unpublished (n.d.), pp. 29, 42 and 72; "The Place of the Book — The Old Testament in the Religion of Jesus," unpublished (n.d.), p. 33; An untitled piece on the Old Testament, unpublished (n.d.), p. 36f.
14. "The Mysticism of the Hebrew Prophets," *At One With The Invisible*, Studies in Mysticism, ed. E. Hershey Sneath (New York: Macmillan, 1921), p. 34: An untitled fragment on the Spirit, *loc. cit.*
15. An untitled fragment on the Spirit, *op. cit.*, p. 21.
16. "Religion of the Spirit," unpublished (n.d.), p. 30f. (To be distinguished from another fragment entitled "The Religion Of The Spirit," unpublished (n.d.). As in so many similar instances, these two fragments are obviously of a piece).
17. "The Historical and the Spiritual Understanding of the Bible," *Education for Christian Service*, by members of the faculty of the Divinity School of Yale University; a volume in commemoration of its one-hundredth anniversary (New Haven: Yale University Press, 1922), pp. 37, 46
18. "Piety and Liberty," *Yale Divinity Quarterly*, VII (November, 1910), p. 49.

19. An untitled fragment on the Spirit, *op. cit.*, p. 4.
20. "Christ the Miracle of Christianity," *The Congregationalist and Christian World* (December 1909), p. 916.
21. *Ibid.*, p. 915.
22. "The Mysticism of the Hebrew Prophets," *op. cit.*, pp. 2, 5, 20, 26, 30.
23. "Historic Facts and Religious Values in the Old Testament," unpublished (n.d.), p. 21f. (To be distinguished from "Historical Facts and Religious Values in the Old Testament").
24. *Biblical Theology of the Old Testament*, unpublished (1923-1924), pp. 25, 27, 36 and 127.
25. *Biblical Theology of the New Testament*, unpublished (1923-1924), p. 66; *New Testament Theology*, unpublished (ca. 1924), p. 106; "Christ the Miracle of Christianity," *op. cit.*, p. 916.
26. Cf. ch. I, n. 2.
27. Review of *Judaism* by George Foote Moore, *The Journal of Religion*, VII, 1, January 1928, pp. 41-43.
28. "A Source-Book of Judaism in New Testament Times," *American Journal of Theology*, XVIII, 1, January 1914, pp. 113-15.
29. "The Sayings of Jesus about the First and the Last," *Journal of Biblical Literature*, XXV, 2 (1906), p. 110; *The Messages of the Apocalyptical Writers* (New York: Charles Scribner's Sons, 1905), p. 68.
30. The Doctrine of Resurrection in Pre-Christian Judaism, *op. cit.*, p. 170f.
31. *New Testament Theology*, *op. cit.*, pp. 64, 67, 110.
32. "Historical Facts and Religious Values in the Old Testament," *op. cit.*, p. 46.
33. Cf. *A Statement of Christian Belief* (New Haven: By the author, 1895), p. 5f.
34. "Some Recent Critical Studies in the Life of Christ," *op. cit.*, pp. 9f., 12.
35. *New Testament Theology: Supplementary Material*, *op. cit.*, p. 28; "The Religion of Jesus," unpublished (n.d.), p. 7; "What Jesus Christ Means to Me," *The Congregationalist and World* CI, 12 (March 23, 1916), p. 396.
36. Hence the impossibility of defining the work of the Spirit in only one way. Cf. "The Spirit of God in the Minds of Men," An address before the New York State Conference of Religion, New York City, November 18, 1902, p. 12.
37. "Toward a Biblical Theology for the Present," *op. cit.*, p. 201.
38. "The Place of the New Testament in the Christian Religion," unpublished (n.d.), p. 9. (To be distinguished from another draft with the same title, but in which all the words are capitalized).
39. "The Place of the Sacred Book in the Christian Religion," *Yale Divinity Quarterly*, V, 4 (March, 1909), p. 265.
40. "The Spirit of Christianity and the Jesus of History," unpublished (n.d.), p. 20.
41. "The Bearing of Historical Studies on the Religious Use of the Bible," *op. cit.*, p. 264.

42. *Biblical Theology of the New Testament, op. cit.*, p. 137.
43. "The Higher Criticism and the Teaching of the Young," *op. cit.*, p. 135; "Historic Fact and Poetic Truth in the Old Testament," unpublished (n.d.), p. 34.
44. "The Place of the Sacred Book in the Christian Religion," *op. cit.*, pp. 262, 265.
45. "The Spirit of Christianity and the Jesus of History," *op. cit.*, p. 16.
46. "The Place of the New Testament in the Christian Religion," *op. cit.*, p. 8; cf. also "The Bearing of Historical Studies on the Religious Use of the Bible," *op. cit., passim.*
47. "Crucial Problems in Biblical Theology," *Journal of Religion*, I, 1 (1921), p. 80; "Some Recent Critical Studies in the Life of Christ," *op. cit.*, p. 1.
48. "Inquiries Concerning the Divinity of Christ," *The American Journal of Theology*, VIII, 1 (January, 1904), p. 19.
49. An untitled piece on the Old Testament, *op. cit.*, p. 36f.
50. "The Minister's Responsibility for the Universality of the Christian Religion," *Yale Divinity Quarterly*, III (January, 1907), pp. 74, 76.
51. "The Jewish Literature of New Testament Times: Why Should it be Studied?" *The Old and New Testament Student*, IX (1889), p. 77.
52. "Ought a Minister to Know Hebrew?" *loc. cit.*
53. "Paul's Belief in Life after Death," *Religion and the Future Life*, ed. E. Hershey Sneath (New York: Fleming Revell, 1922), p. 238.
54. "The Bearing of Historical Studies on the Religious Use of the Bible," *op. cit.*, p. 259.
55. "The Place of the Sacred Book in the Christian Religion," *op. cit.*, p. 262.
56. "The Bearing of Historical Studies on the Religious Use of the Bible," *op. cit.*, pp. 262, 272; "Religious Fellowship, Its Basis, Bounds, and Bane," *Getting Together*, Essays by Friends in Council on the Regulative Ideals of Religious Thought, ed. James M. Whiton (New York: Sturgis and Walton Co., 1913), p. 12; cf. "Religion of the Spirit," *op. cit.*, pp. 24ff.
57. "Historic Fact and Poetic Truth in the Old Testament," *op. cit.*, pp. 6f., 34, 56, 59; "The Place of the New Testament in the Christian Religion," *op. cit.*, pp. 11, 20.
58. "The Place of the Sacred Book in the Christian Religion," *op. cit.*, p. 264.
59. *Biblical Theology of the Old Testament, op. cit.*, p. 26.
60. "Historic Fact and Poetic Truth in the Old Testament," *op. cit.*, p. 4.
61. "The Place Of The New Testament In The Christian Religion," unpublished (n.d.), pp. 12f., 26.
62. *New Testament Theology, op cit.*, p. 41.
63. *Biblical Theology of the Old Testament, op. cit.*, p. 26.
64. "The Place of the Sacred Book in the Christian Religion, *op. cit.*, p. 264; "Historic Fact and Poetic Truth in the Old Testament," *op. cit.*, pp. 9-12, 16, 19, 20; Aristotle, *On Poetry and Music*, trans. S. H. Butcher

(New York: The Bobbs-Merrill Co., Inc., 1956), p. 13, and *Wordsworth's Prefaces and Essays on Poetry*, ed. A. J. George (Boston: D. C. Heath & Co., 1892).

65. "Historic Fact and Poetic Truth in the Old Testament," *op. cit.*, pp. 11-14, 16, 47.

66. Longinus, *On Great Writing* (On the Sublime), trans. G. M. A.Grube (New York: The Liberal Arts Press, 1957).

67. *Ibid.*, pp. 10, 12.

68. "Historic Fact and Poetic Truth in the Old Testament," *op. cit.*, p. 25; cf. pp. 20-21, 26.

69. "The Bearing of Historical Studies on the Religious Use of the Bible," *op. cit.*, p. 276.

70. "Peking Address," *op. cit.*, p. 3.

71. "Our Rights and Duties as to the Bible," unpublished (n.d.), p. 1; cf. "The Historical and the Spiritual Understanding of the Bible," *op. cit.*, p. 28.

72. "The Place Of The New Testament In The Christian Religion," *op. cit.*, p. 124.

73. *Ibid.*, p. 82.

74. *Wordsworth's Prefaces and Essays on Poetry, op. cit.*, p. 15f.; cf. "Historic Fact and Poetic Truth in the Old Testament," *op. cit.*, 29f.

75. "Historic Fact and Poetic Truth in the Old Testament," *op. cit.*, pp. 15, 30, 60, 64.

76. *Ibid.*, p. 65f.

77. *Biblical Theology of the New Testament, op. cit.*, p. 18.

78. *The Mind of Christ in Paul*, Light from Paul on present Problems of Christian Thinking (New York: Charles Scribner's Sons, 1930), pp. 9, 11; "The Intellectual Value of Theological Training," *op. cit.*, p. 8.

79. *The Mind of Christ in Paul, op. cit.*, p. 9f.; cf. also p. 11f.; "The Intellectual Value of Theological Training," *loc. cit.*; "Peking Address," *op. cit.*, p. 4; "Dr. Timothy Dwight as a New Testament Scholar," unpublished (n.d.), p. 7; *Biblical Theology of the New Testament, op. cit.*, p. 18.

80. "Dr. Timothy Dwight as a New Testament Scholar," *op. cit.*, p. 6.

81. "What Jesus Christ Means to Me," *op. cit.*, p. 396.

82. "Problems Old and New," unpublished (n.d.), p. 3.

83. Comments found in Porter's copy of Rudolf Bultmann's *Jesus and the Word*.

84. "Toward a Biblical Theology for the Present," *op. cit.*, pp. 200, 234f.

85. *The Mind of Christ in Paul, op. cit.*, p. 8.

86. "The Historical and the Spiritual Understanding of the Bible," *op. cit.*, p. 23.

87. "Christ the Miracle of Christianity," *op. cit.*, p. 915; *A Statement of Christian Belief, op. cit.*, p. 3.

88. Cf. "Toward a Biblical Theology for the Present," *op. cit.*, p. 201; *New Testament Theology, op. cit.*, p. 67.

89. "Historic Fact and Poetic Truth in the Old Testament," *op. cit.*, p. 42.
90. "The Sayings of Jesus about the First and the Last," *op. cit.*, p. 109f.
91. *New Testament Theology, op. cit.*, p. 67.
92. "The Signs of God in the Life of Man," *Modern Sermons by World Scholars*, ed. Robert Scott and William C. Stiles (New York: Funk and Wagnalls, 1909), VII, 208; *A Statement of Christian Belief, op. cit.*, p. 3.
93. "Religious Fellowship, Its Basis, Bounds, and Bane," *op. cit.*, p. 10; "Toward a Biblical Theology for the Present," *op. cit.*, p. 205.
94. *Biblical Theology of the Old Testament, op, cit ,* pp. 49, 52-54.
95. *New Testament Theology, op. cit.*, p. 64.
96. "A Suggesion regarding Isaiah's Immanuel," *Journal of Biblical Literature*, XIV (1895); *Biblical Theology of the Old Testament, op. cit.*, p. 60f.; "Historic Facts and Religious Values in the Old Testament," *op. cit.*, p. 25f.
97. *Biblical Theology of the Old Testament, op. cit.*, p. 95; "Historic Facts and Religious Values in the Old Testament," *op. cit.*, p. 24.
98. *Biblical Theology of the Old Testament, op. cit.*, pp. 27, 110; *New Testament Theology: Supplementary Material, op. cit.*, p. 14; "Religious Fellowship, Its Basis, Bounds, and Bane," *op. cit.*, p. 8; "History of Biblical Conceptions: Revelation and Inspiration," unpublished, (1923-1924), p. 9.
99. "History of Biblical Conceptions: Hellenistic Judaism," unpublished (1923-1924), p. 3; an untitled piece on the Old Testament, *op. cit.*, p. 30.
100. "The Religion of the Spirit," *op. cit.*, p. 42; "Historic Fact and Poetic Truth in the Old Testament," *op. cit.*, p. 26.
101. An untitled piece on the Old Testament, *op. cit.*, p. 34.
102. "The Place of the Book — The Old Testament in the Religion of Jesus," *op. cit.*, p. 38.
103. At the same time, he thought he detected a fundamental inconsistency in Bultmann's parable-interpretation, viz., an exclusion of the present kingship of Jahveh and yet an affirmation of present kingship; a spiritualizing of Jesus' teachings and yet a naturalizing of the Gospels, cf. comments found in Porter's copy of Bultmann's *Jesus and the Word, loc. cit.*
104. "Historic Fact and Poetic Truth in the Old Testament," *op. cit.*, p. 45.
105. *New Testament Theology: Supplementary Material, op. cit.*, p. 20; "The Place Of The New Testament In The Christian Religion," *op. cit.*, p. 57.
106. *Biblical Theology of the New Testament, op. cit.*, pp. 30, 53, 62; *New Testament Theology, op. cit.*, pp. 85, 89f.
107. "The Place of the Book — The Old Testament in the Religion of Jesus," *op. cit.*, p. 49f.; "The Place of the New Testament in the Christian Religion," *op. cit.*, p. 21f; "Things Greater and Less in the Bible," *Yale Divinity Quarterly* (March, 1911), pp. 117, 122; "Toward a Biblical Theology for the Present," *op. cit.*, p. 227f.

44

108. *Biblical Theology of the New Testament, op. cit.*, p. 108; *New Testament Theology, op. cit.*, pp. 23, 103; "History of Biblical Conceptions: Christology," unpublished (1924), p. 21f.
109. *Biblical Theology of the New Testament, op. cit.*, p. 136; "History of Biblical Conceptions: Christology," *op. cit.*, pp. 21, 28. Porter was equally critical of Martin Kähler's insistence that the Gospels are confessions of faith, not records of fact and that faith is thus the only historical fact to be sought. He wrote that Kähler's position failed to meet the condition of a true "return" to the historical Jesus. He noted also the emphases of Catholic modernists and Protestants who construed Christianity as a certain truth or ideal and Jesus as its historical originator and permanent symbol. Porter stated that the approach of Albert Loisy, who sought for the essence of this ideal in the development of the church was too abstract — it affirmed the liberty, but did not inspire the reverence with which the Christian stands in the presence of Jesus Christ. Of Otto Pfleiderer's attempt to apprehend the truth of Christ in the philosophical and ethical ideals to which human development had carried men, Porter wrote that it was "too unideal" in its concreteness. On the other hand, though approving the Ritschlian view and that of Wilhelm Herrmann to the effect that by moral and religious experience we attain to a picture of Jesus' inner life which in turn convinces us of his historical actuality, Porter criticized it for its "exclusiveness," its insistence that Jesus as fact must displace Jesus as symbol. This exclusiveness, Porter stated, could only be justified if the historical Jesus were completely identified with the idea of universality and spirituality in religion. Since the Ritschlian would by no means consent to such an identification, he also failed to meet the condition for a true "return." Cf. *Biblical Theology of the New Testament, op. cit.*, p. 23; "Religious Fellowship, Its Basis, Bounds, and Bane," *op. cit.*, p. 19f.; "The Spirit of Christianity and the Jesus of History," *op. cit.*, pp. 21, 23f., 30, 32f., 35, 38, 56-58.
110. "Paul's Belief in Life after Death," *op. cit.*, p. 254.
111. *The Mind of Christ in Paul, op. cit.*, p. 20; "Paul and the Spirit of God," unpublished (n.d.), p. 19; "The Place of Apocalyptic Conceptions in the Thought of Paul," *Journal of Biblical Literature*, XLI (1922), pp. 197, 199. Porter described the New Testament literature as reflecting a dual movement away from Christ's physical return. The one, at home in "Q," Mark, Matthew and Revelation, emphasized the individual's life after death. The other accented the ethical. The latter, wrote Porter, was the more characteristic of New Testament religion, and Paul its greatest exponent. It was Paul who profoundly changed the meaning of traditional apocalyptic ideas by "spiritualizing" them. That spiritualizing consisted in transferring his personal experience of Jesus to his conception of the coming world. In other words, apocalyptic was Paul's vehicle for interpreting historical

PRINCIPLES OF INTERPRETATION

events in the life of Christ. The first consequence of such spiritualizing was that the new age was seen as having already appeared, the second the idea that the man in Christ would more fully attain to immortality. The apparent contradiction between these two notions, said Porter, could be resolved by way of a proper understanding of Romans 8, according to which the future brings the transformation of the physical or outward world into its destined fullness for the spiritual and inward life already achieved. The resurrection is thus simply an extrapolation of the Christian's oneness with Christ — it is that event by which Spirit has entered human life, the last and final place of the individual determined by the nature of love. Cf. "The Christian Hope in Times of War," *Religion and the War*, by members of the faculty of the School of Religion, Yale University, ed. E. Hershey Sneath (New Haven: Yale University Press, 1918), p. 48; "The Place of Apocalyptical Conceptions in the Thought of Paul," *op. cit.*, pp. 183f., 191; "The Religion Of The Spirit," *op. cit.*, p. 35; *New Testament Theology*, *op. cit.*, p. 130; *The Mind of Christ in Paul*, *op. cit.*, p. 311; *Biblical Theology of the New Testament*, *op. cit.*, p. 137; "Paul's Belief in Life After Death," *op. cit.*, pp. 233, 256, 258.

112. "The Spirit of Christianity and the Jesus of History," *op. cit.*, pp. 61, 65, 72.
113. *The Mind of Christ in Paul*, *op. cit.*, p. 95f.
114. *Ibid.*, pp. 133, 139.
115. "Toward a Biblical Theology for the Present," *op. cit.*, p. 238.
116. "History of Biblical Conceptions: Christology," *op. cit.*, p. 27.
117. Untitled piece on things greater and less in the New Testament, *op. cit.*, p. 6; *The Mind of Christ in Paul*, *op. cit.*, p. 241.
118. "Christian Thinking about Christ," unpublished (n.d.), p. 10f.; *The Mind of Christ in Paul*, *op. cit.*, pp. 119, 172-80, 182, 187.
119. *The Mind of Christ in Paul*, *op. cit.*, pp. 180f., 187, 197; "Christian Thinking about Christ," *op. cit.*, p. 12.
120. "The Place Of The New Testament In The Christian Religion," *op. cit.*, pp. 13f., 25; *The Mind of Christ in Paul*, *op. cit.*, pp. 170, 204, 208, 215, 271; "Christian Thinking about Christ," *op. cit.*, pp. 15-17.
121. "The Place Of The New Testament In The Christian Religion," *op. cit.*, pp. 6, 8, 10; *The Mind of Christ in Paul*, *op. cit.*, p. 163; "Paul and the Spirit of God," *op. cit.*, p. 43.
122. *New Testament Theology: Supplementary Material*, *op. cit.*, p. 24; *Biblical Theology of the New Testament*, *op. cit.*, p. 136f.; *The Mind of Christ in Paul*, *op. cit.*, p. 80.
123. *New Testament Theology: Supplementary Material*, *op. cit.*, p. 20; *The Mind of Christ in Paul*, *op. cit.*, pp. 81, 87f., 282, 288, 312; "History of Biblical Conceptions: Christology," *op. cit.*, p. 33; "Interpreters of the Bible and Discoverers of God," Commencement Address, 1924, *Yale Divinity News* (November, 1924), p. 9; *New Testament Theology*, *op. cit.*, p. 138.

124. *New Testament Theology, op. cit.*, p. 138; *New Testament Theology: Supplementary Material, op. cit.*, p. 20; "Christian Thinking about Christ," *op. cit.*, p. 15; *The Mind of Christ in Paul, op. cit.*, pp. 55f., 78, 81, 85, 87, 239, 290, 296, 311; Shorthand review of Theodore Munger's biography of Horace Bushnell, *op. cit.*, p. 2; "The Religion Of The Spirit," *op. cit.*, p. 35, 37.

125. *The Mind of Christ in Paul, op. cit.*, p. 260f.

126. "Inquiries Concerning the Divinity of Christ," *op. cit.*, pp. 13f., 18; "The Sufficiency of the Religion of Jesus," *The American Journal of Theology*, XI, 1 (January, 1907), pp. 88, 90; An untitled piece on things greater and less in the New Testament, *op. cit.*, p. 4f.; *Biblical Theology of the New Testament, op. cit.*, pp. 115f., 122.

127. *New Testament Theology, op. cit.*, pp. 44, 50, 106; *Biblical Theology of the New Testament, op. cit.*, pp. 71, 100; "Toward a Biblical Theology for the Present," *op. cit.*, p. 225.

128. "Christian Thinking about Christ," *op. cit.*, pp. 2, 11, 15.

129. "The Religion Of The Spirit," *op. cit.*, p. 31f.; *New Testament Theology, op. cit.*, p. 138; *The Mind of Christ in Paul, op. cit.*, p. 298f.

130. *The Mind of Christ in Paul, op. cit.*, p. 81.

131. Cf. "The Place of Christ in the Christian Religion," unpublished (n.d.), pp. 69f., 76.

132. "The Place of the Sacred Book in the Christian Religion," *op. cit.*, p. 260; "The Religion Of The Spirit," *op. cit.*, p. 41.

133. *New Testament Theology, op. cit.*, p. 60; "The Problem of Things New and Old in the Beginnings of Christianity," *Journal of Biblical Literature*, XLVIII (1929), 20; "Christian Thinking about Christ, *op. cit.*, pp. 6f., 18.

134. "Interpreters of the Bible and Discoverers of God," *op. cit.*, p. 11f.; *The Mind of Christ in Paul, op. cit.*, p. 48.

135. "The Spirit of God in the Minds of Men," *op. cit.*, p. 5; *The Mind of Christ in Paul, op. cit.*, pp. 46f., 71, 85; An untitled fragment on the Fourth Gospel, unpublished (n.d.), p. 1f.; "The Problem," unpublished (n.d.), pp. 5, 17; "The Religion Of The Spirit," *op. cit.*, pp. 15, 23, 35f., 41; *New Testament Theology, op. cit.*, p. 110; "Toward a Biblical Theology for the Present," *op. cit.*, p. 237.

136. "The Place Of The New Testament In The Christian Religion," *op. cit.*, p. 59f.

137. *Ibid.*; cf. "How Well Do We Need to Know the Life of Christ?" *The Congregationalist* (September, 1894), p. 375.

138. "The Place of Christ in the Christian Religion," *op. cit.*, p. 79f.

139. "The Religion Of The Spirit," *op. cit.*, pp. 15ff.

140. *Ibid.*

141. *New Testament Theology, op. cit.*, p. 24; An untitled fragment on the Fourth Gospel, *op. cit.*, p. 15f.

142. "The Religion Of The Spirit," *op. cit.*, pp. 28f., 46.

143. A sermon preached on John 20:29 (1886–1887).

144. "Inquiries Concerning the Divinity of Christ," *op. cit.*, p. 22.
145. "The Place of Christ in the Christian Religion," *op. cit.*, p. 82; An untitled fragment on the Fourth Gospel, *op. cit.*, p. 4f.
146. "The Place Of The New Testament In The Christian Religion," *op. cit.*, p. 63; "The Place of Christ in the Christian Religion," *op. cit.*, p. 82.
147. An untitled fragment on the Fourth Gospel, *op. cit.*, p. 2.
148. "History of Biblical Conceptions: Christology," *op. cit.*, p. 20; "Paul and the Spirit of God," *op. cit.*, p. 14; "The Signs of God in the Life of Man," *op. cit.*, p. 191.
149. "History of Biblical Conceptions: Christology," *loc. cit.*; "The Religion Of The Spirit," *op. cit.*, p. 12f.
150. Earlier, Porter had written that the physical operation of the Spirit was almost negligible, cf. "History of Biblical Conceptions: Christology," *loc. cit.*
151. "The Problem," *op. cit.*, p. 7; An untitled fragment on the Spirit, *op. cit.*, p. 9.
152. Fragment on eschatology and the supernatural, unpublished (n.d.).
153. "On the Spirit," unpublished (n.d.), p. 16.
154. "The Word of God and the Spirit of God," unpublished (n.d.), p. 20.
155. "The Religious and the Historical Uses of the Bible," *The New World*, III, 10 (June, 1894), p. 258; "The Bearing of Historical Studies on the Religious Use of the Bible," *op. cit.*, pp. 253-76; "Toward a Biblical Theology for the Present," *op. cit.*, p. 216.
156. "The Place Of The New Testament In The Christian Religion," *op. cit.*, pp. 29f., 94.
157. "The Religious and the Historical Uses of the Bible," *op. cit.*, pp. 251-55.
158. "Ought a Minister to Know Hebrew?" *op. cit.*, p. 633. At times, Porter cited Wordsworth's "classical description" of the function of poetry in its relation to science, writing that in regard to questions of bare fact, religious experience could hardly be allowed to take the lead and go forward alone to the end. Cf. "Toward a Biblical Theology for the Present," *op. cit.*, p. 219; "The Bearing of Historical Studies on the Religious Use of the Bible," *op. cit.*, pp. 266, 269.
159. "Inquiries Concerning the Divinity of Christ," *op. cit.*, p. 27.
160. "The Liberal and the Ritschlian Theology of Germany," *op. cit.*, pp. 458, 460.
161. "Inquiries Concerning the Divinity of Christ," *op. cit.*, p. 28.
162. "The Religious and the Historical Uses of the Bible," *op. cit.*, pp. 255f., 258-60.
163. "The Historical and the Spiritual Understanding of the Bible," *op. cit.*, p. 22; "Toward a Biblical Theology for the Present," *op. cit.*, p. 216; "The Word of God and the Spirit of God," *op. cit.*, p. 20f.
164. "Toward a Biblical Theology for the Present," *op. cit.*, p. 210.
165. "The Word of God and the Spirit of God," *op. cit.*, p. 21.

166. An untitled piece on the Old Testament, *op. cit.*, p. 56; "The Religious and the Historical Uses of the Bible," *op. cit.*, p. 260.
167. An untitled piece on the Old Testament, *op. cit.*, p. 55.
168. "The Place Of The New Testament In The Christian Religion," *op. cit.*, pp. 29, 48.
169. "The Religious and the Historical Uses of the Bible," *op. cit.*, p. 257.
170. "Historic Fact and Poetic Truth in the Old Testament," *op. cit.*, p. 53.
171. "The Bearing of Historical Studies on the Religious Use of the Bible," *op. cit.*, p. 275.
172. Letter to Mr. Chas. Wingate, July 19, 1896.
173. "The Place Of The New Testament In The Christian Religion," *op. cit.*, p. 104.
174. *Ibid.*, p. 92.
175. *Ibid.*, p. 109.

CHAPTER THREE

EVALUATION

Introduction:

Porter's work was variously evaluated by his contemporaries, and of these evaluations the majority treated only aspects of his thought and not the whole of it. R. H. Charles and John D. Davis of Princeton noted the similarity between Porter's treatment of Old and New Testament apocalyptic and the methods of the History of Religions School.[1] According to W. D. Davies, Porter's volume on Paul had set him in a class with Baur and Holtzmann, had rendered him incapable of an objective interpretation of the great Christological passages and reflected an anti-metaphysical, anti-substantialist bias.[2] A friend, James Everett Frame of Union Theological Seminary in New York, suggested that Porter's personalistic resolution of the paradox "Christ in us" and "we in Christ" need not have excluded the "substantial," and concluded that Porter had tried to give Paul a theological consistency which ran athwart his intention to assign the apostle a religious consistency, an attempt, he added, which was highly reminiscent of Albert Schweitzer.[3] Burton Scott Easton wrote that Porter's pursuit of his method recalled those good, old Scottish theologians who could prove Paul a supralapsarian at every turn, insisted that the ethics of Paul did indeed imply a "metaphysic", noted Porter's idealistic conception of Paul's relation to Christ together with his *imitatio* Christology, and laid the blame for it all on Albrecht Ritschl.[4] Morton Scott Enslin, however, was happy to attribute such bias to Porter and revelled in it.[5] But the net result for most was summed up by Harold Willoughby – either Porter had modernized Paul beyond all recognition or he possessed a religion without a theology.[6]

This does not mean Porter went unthanked for his pains.
The letters and correspondence contained in that rabbit
warren of his files give witness to the envy and praise of his
contemporaries on both continents. Leipoldt, Kittel,
Windisch, Oesterly, Dodd and Odeberg shared his criticism
of George Foote Moore's inattention to Jewish apocalyptic.
Erwin R. Goodenough wrote that Porter's review of Moore's
Judaism was the best review of any book he had ever read.[7]
Even W. D. Davies conceded that Porter's work in this area
had returned apocalyptic to mainstream Judaism where it
belonged. Praise for his work poured out of letters from
Shirley Jackson Case of Chicago, Ernest Hocking of
Harvard, Ernest Findlay Scott of Union in New York and
James Muilenberg, then of Mount Holyoke. In all of it,
however, there is little which allows us to get at the core of
the man.

An attempt to fit what came from Porter's pen to the grid
of such characterizations as are found, for example, in
Wieman and Meland's *American Philosophies of Religion*
would produce only a Duke's mixture. What is said there of
the aesthetic naturalist, the absolutist, the mystic, the
personalist, the ethical intuitionist, the liberal, romanticist,
pragmatist, eclectical and moral optimist could conceivably
be applied to Porter.[8] Porter shared interests and passions
with all or many of these types, but how to get at the spring
and motive of his thought?

A letter from H. Richard Niebuhr to Roland Bainton, in
response to the latter's unpublished portrait of Porter,[9]
suggests some point of beginning from which to evaluate
him. In reply to Bainton's suggestion that Porter had been
deeply influenced by Jonathan Edwards and three New
England themes — the Reformation, the Enlightenment
and Pietism "tinged" with Romanticism — Niebuhr wrote:

> I think New Testament piety is here *transformed* by what may be
> called Romanticism but what was more a "Platonistically"
> transformed Romanticism. Porter is directly descended from
> Coleridge. All these things he has to say about poetry and about
> the emotional grasping of objects that must be fashioned and
> shaped by imagination even while they are known in their

objective reality — this is pure Coleridge. Coleridge reenacted rather than reproduced. And this Coleridgeanism blends with the Platonism in Edwards and that whole strain in English thought. It's a far cry from Dwight. But near Bushnell. . . .[10]

I: *Porter and Edwards Compared*:

The reference to Edwards is suggestive. Edwards occupied as large a place as any other in the published and unpublished pieces of Porter. More important, those works which refer to Edwards are either close to the center of Porter's scholarly concern or are of the nature of personal testimony. Edwards has his place in Porter's attempt to gather Christians and Jews beneath the universal of divine and infinite love.[11] He appears in "What Jesus Christ Means to Me" and writings of similar genre.[12] The unpublished lectures on Biblical Theology and their supplements; the commencement address delivered at Yale and *The Mind of Christ in Paul*; his voluminous notes on the publications of his colleague Bacon, notes found in his volume of Bultmann's *Jesus and the Word* and on Theodore Munger's biography of Horace Bushnell — all make reference to Edwards. From 1913 on, there is constant appeal to the New England theologian. But this would be of little consequence if we could not uncover some instance in which Porter acknowledged his dependence upon Edwards for some key concept or strategic point on which his thought is made to rest.

The acknowledgment appears in what was really the only book Porter ever wrote — *The Mind of Christ in Paul*. At the base of his interpretation of the apostle lay Edwards' posthumously published "Treatise on Grace." Porter acknowledged it flat outright — Edwards had described Paul's idea of Christ, the Christian and the relation between them better than anyone else. What was left was merely to restate what Edwards had written long ago, i.e., that the "very quintessence of all Religion, the very thing wherein lies summarily the sincerity, spirituality, and divinity of Religion, is LOVE."[13]

If Porter's acknowledged dependence upon Edwards furnishes us a clue, then it is legitimate to ask what else these two, separated by two hundred years, shared in common, and wherein they differed.

From an examination of the writings of both, it is clear, first of all, that both Edwards and Porter were engaged in a struggle to unite. According to his interpreters, the question for Edwards was that of uniting two apparently hostile worlds, symbolized by the names of Newton and Locke — the world of the mechanical and the world of conscious thought. Edwards spent his life in an attempt to forge harmony out of what has been termed the contrast between "the objective good" as the "irresistible sequence of law" and the "inherent good" as the "perception of excellency or pleasure," or, out of what a more recent study describes as the contrast between "beauty and sensibility."[14] It was an age-old antinomy with which Edwards, the first "theologian of mediation" in this country, was wrestling.

This struggle with the "two gigantic issues of modern philosophy" lay at the heart of Porter's work as well. Naturally, he translated the problem into his own coin and in ways which often separated him from Edwards. For Porter, the mediation had to be found between "history and religion,"[15] between the "outward, objective elements in religion and the inward,"[16] between "wonder and transport," science and faith, a contrast signalized in the conflict between the so-called Ritschlian and liberal theological schools. Porter's address to the New York State Conference on Religion, for all its idealistic cast, was as clear a formulation of the problem as he had ever given:

> We need the concrete, the peculiar, the special, the sensible, to make real to us and to bring within our reach the God of all and the universal good in which we would share. But there is danger that the definite and the particular, because it is our own, will shut us off from the whole, rather than secure it for us and introduce us into it. Whenever our particular religion cultivates in us the love which is toward others hate, the danger has been realized and the good lost. Yet to seek with the philosopher to let the particular go and cleave to the universal alone, is to attempt what few can attain. There must therefore be a way in which the universal and the particular elements can interact upon each other, the particular keep the universal from being far off and insecure and

unattainable, and the universal keep the particular from being
narrow and divisive . . . Jonathan Edwards in his essay on the
Nature of True Virtue has made quite the same distinction
between selective earthly love and impartial heavenly love.[17]

Contending that religion required founding in the total
person, that such understanding of God and man as New
England theology had always construed it excluded
experience and was thus doomed to abstraction, Edwards
wrote that

if we take reason strictly, not for the faculty of mental perception
in general, but for ratiocination . . . the perceiving of spiritual
beauty and excellency no more belongs to reason than it belongs
to the sense of feeling to perceive colors. . . . Reason may
determine that a countenance is beautiful to others, it may
determine that honey is sweet to others; but it will never give me a
perception of its sweetness.[18]

Porter's quarrel was the same — the reason scientific
research could not furnish the basis for religious uses was not
only that "a certain insecurity" attended all the results of
historical study,[19] but also that rationality was but one
aspect of genuine religion. The conclusion could only be that
doctrine or theological speculation was no substitute for
religion. To his Harvard opponents and others of the same
mind, Edwards responded that "he that has doctrinal
knowledge and speculation only . . . never is engaged in the
business of religion."[20] And Porter deplored what he alleged
to be the contention of his Princeton adversaries, viz., that a
knowledge of Christ's death apart from the perception of its
ethical character and effect constituted a true faith.[21]
Occasionally, Porter would appeal to Yale's "second
founder," Timothy Dwight the elder, a man never known to
lay cavalier hands on the traditional dogma, but for whom
dogma "was only an expression of the fact that in the
contemplation of Jesus and in fellowship and friendship with
him men find eternal life."[22]

For neither Edwards nor Porter did the refusal to give
priority to the rational imply a disparagement of its proper
place in the religious life. On the contrary, Edwards, in
opposition to most revivalists, contended that a man was

required to understand as well as hear and regarded that sense of beauty and excellence which was to achieve the synthesis between the mechanical and the conscious as removing reason's hindrances and as a positive aid.[23] Porter, too, pressed home the necessity of keeping faith abreast of present knowledge, above all for the sake of those who could not agree to the claims of a religion expressed in unintelligible language.[24] Indeed, both were sanguine enough respecting the results of biblical study to assume that whatever such study uncovered as the essence of the Christian faith would commend itself to reason. Edwards wrote:

> It is a glorious argument of the divinity of the holy Scriptures that they teach such doctrines . . . which . . . when they are most carefully and strictly examined, appear to be exactly agreeable to the most demonstrable, certain and natural dictates of reason.[25]

Porter insisted that what was most distinctive and characteristic in Jesus' teaching was that which the historical critic must recognize as most important.[26] Porter, heir to what Edwards could not be — a long history of critical biblical research — was even willing to turn that sentence round to read that such distinctions in the New Testament as are made by historical study justify themselves to religious experience.[27]

Edwards as well as Porter saw the synthesis of the two opposing worlds in what can only be termed the aesthetic factor. For Edwards it was beauty which achieved the union between sensation and thought, the objective and the subjective, between the structured order in the world and human experience. That beauty was perceived in the "affections," in "fervent exercises of the heart," in that "sense" of the comeliness of the divine or in a new "taste" or "spiritual sensation" — something of which the "devils and damned in hell are, and for ever will be, entirely destitute."[28] Whether or not this aspect of Edwards' thought has been missed or minimized until now, and to what degree it introduces a novel element into Augustinian tradition,[29] the contention of his recent interpreters is that this aesthetic-affectional side of his thought constitutes the distinctive and principle mark of Edwards' philosophical theology.[30]

There is that same aesthetic-affective aspect to Porter's thought: "wonder and worship, trust and love, naturally express themselves in the language of feeling, the language of poetry, not in that of explanation and definition."[31] The hands may be those of Esau, Longinus, Arnold, Wordsworth or Coleridge, but the voice is that of Jacob — the similarity to Edwards is unmistakable. And so is Porter's appraisal of the language of the Bible as "poetic," as stirring the heart and kindling the imagination, as making its proper appeal through the feelings, its truths "carried alive into the heart by passion."[32] Porter had merely applied to Scripture itself Edwards' recommendation of books "as have a tendency deeply to affect the hearts of those who attend these means."[33] And, some attention to Porter's style will be enough to convince the reader that if Edwards was able by his affective style to compel the reader to understand "by vicarious participation in what is being described,"[34] Porter had gifts in the same direction, though his wife at least once sighed, "if only Frank could write."[35] There is nothing in Porter, perhaps, to match the spider-analogy in Edwards' Enfield sermon, but his prose was mellifluous enough.

It was Porter's contention that "insight and sympathy" or a "sense" into the beauty and truth of Jesus' words was of greater value than any "eternally self-verifying religion *about* Jesus" which his colleague Bacon might defend.[36] The bent was clearly Edwardsean, reflecting the Northhampton preacher's demand for a direct and immediate apprehension of Christ which resulted in giving priority to beauty over sensibility.[37] In neither Edwards nor Porter was this aesthetic synthesis without its practical or ethical side. If Edwards had regarded beauty as determining both reality and value, as providing the key to both being and goodness,[38] and had written that "virtue is the beauty of those qualities and acts of the mind, that are of a *moral* nature,"[39] Porter thought it no great departure to affirm with Keats that "'beauty is truth, truth beauty' — that is all ye know on earth, and all ye need to know." Again, Porter

argued that the radicalism of the Bible consists in the
substitution of a new character and its outcome in conduct
for the ideas and usages of traditional religion.[40] He stated
that the "new religion" was not a mere receiving but an
achieving as well;[41] that the will to make Christ's death our
own in character and conduct was the "greater thing."[42]
Assigning such "fusion of morals and religion" to the great
prophets and to Jesus, and seeing in it the distinguishing
mark and peculiar virtue of biblical religion,[43] Porter was
willing to conclude that to the degree Christ's company of
followers exalted him, fitted him out with lofty titles such as
qualitatively separated him from them, to that degree they
had exempted themselves from a like existence with his:

> They were wrong, when they assumed that it was enough to see
> God in him. That they had no further and consequent duty to see
> God with him in the world and in men. Wrong so far as they
> thought he had done all that men had to do in order to prove that
> truth.[44]

The stimulus certainly lay with Edwards who exhorted a
man to pay attention to his behavior, demanded that the
biblical rule and precept be supplemented with the empirical
act and described the "deed" as "chief of all the signs of
grace."[45] "Herein chiefly appears the power of true
godliness," Edwards had said, "viz., in its being effectual in
practice."[46] And Edwards' numerous references to duty in
his "Resolutions" and Diary[47] could have earned him the
same criticism as Bacon aimed at the "religion of Jesus" and
hence at Porter, signalized in what Bacon had called the
paternalistic theism of the Sermon on the Mount and the
Lord's Prayer. If Edwards was "subordinating the
traditional 'immanent grace' to the power of the Spirit as
expressed in overt behavior,"[48] so was Porter.

That *imitatio* piety which Easton believed he detected in
Porter was not foreign to Edwards. Porter identified "the
religion of the Spirit" with "reproduction."[49] He described
the Christology of the New Testament as greater than later
church dogma because it included the "real imitation" of

Christ by the disciple.[50] He called his reader to look more intently upon Christ so as to be transformed into the same likeness,[51] called him not only to feel as Paul felt but to do what he did.[52] Edwards, too, had insisted that "'tis by a sight of the beauty and amiableness of God's holiness that the heart is transformed into the same image and strongly engaged to imitate God."[53]

For Edwards, beauty was of the essence of the divine and the model for all being.[54] Indeed, nature and the human body with it were regarded as an emanation of the divine beauty:

> The beauties of nature are really emantions or shadows of the excellence of the Son of God. . . . In like manner, when we behold the beauty of man's body, in its perfection, we still see like emanations of Christ's divine perfections.[55]

The finite could bear the infinite; Spirit could be manifest in the created, natural world; the world's beauty could be a "substantial" communication of the beauty of God.[56] In Edwards there was what Perry Miller called that weaving of the supernatural into the natural which "made the mystery so nearly comprehensible that it became terrifying."[57] And the conclusion Porter drew was that the supernatural was to be found within the natural and nowhere else.[58] Porter's rejection of the cultic, the sacramental;[59] his interpretation of Jesus' temptation as reflecting resistance to externality and intervention; his excluding from Jesus' miracles the category of the prodigious; his identification of Spirit with immanence and his consequent criticism of the view of dialectical theology as "out of all harmony with our view of the world"[60] — all this certainly cannot be explained in terms of Porter's dependence upon Edwards, but it does justify our assuming Edwards furnished a certain stimulus. What Porter described as the religion of his contemporaries could, with some qualification, have been said of Edwards:

> Through the work of physical science we have come to an altogether new understanding and to an altogether new control of the physical world. Our knowledge of nature leads us to expect

everywhere and always an orderly and intelligible sequence of causes and effects. . . . That God is about us and within us, that he does not act by miracle as from without but penetrates the universe as its ultimate energy and its guiding reason and that he dwells in men as the source of life, and of the higher life of truth and beauty and goodness, this faith in the environing and indwelling God, may claim to be the religion of the modern man.[61]

The question is not whether Edwards could hold to such continuity between nature and grace. The question is rather whether Porter, like Edwards, could truly affirm immanence, or due to some alien commitment could do so only with tongue in cheek.

From the affirmation of such continuity, it was but a short step for Edwards to ascribe universality to beauty and to such degree that he exalted it above being as such and resolved the very being of God himself into it.[62] Porter contended that his definition of religion as search for the universal[63] merely reflected Edwards' distinction between selective, earthly love and impartial heavenly love as expounded in "The Nature of True Virtue,"[64] and he appealed to Edwards' idea of love as denoting the "sense" or "perception of *value* in all men."[65] Against this background, Porter's predilection for the wisdom literature of Judaism[66] his occasional description of Jesus as a wisdom teacher, "revelling" in "The Writings,"[67] and finally his attempt to establish a connection between Paul and the Book of Wisdom,[68] are at least partly explained.

Since for Edwards and for Porter true religion was a matter of the "affections," simple, common folk could apprehend it. Edwards stated that common people were "furthest from having their thoughts perverted from their natural channel, by metaphysical and philosophical subtelties."[69] Porter embraced "the spirit of democracy" because it reflected Christ's reverence for every common human being,[70] his love for the common people.[71] He interpreted the parables after the fashion of Adolf Jülicher because he was convinced the Kingdom came in "lowly common ordinary gradual" goings on.[72] He wrote that the truths which Jesus taught were more easily understood by the childlike than by the wise[73] and repudiated the Princetonian, orthodox view of the Bible as an obstacle to conceiving the Divine Spirit in common as well as uncommon events.[74] The Bible, Porter said, rather belongs to that species of literature which makes common things "reveal unnoticed and rare beauties and truths."[75] And when it came to a choice between the evangelists who narrated facts of a unique character and Jesus who taught men to see the goodness of God in common things and human nature,[76] Porter chose the latter, the "religion of Jesus."[77] Just as Edwards had contended there was no need that the "strict philosophic truth should be at all concealed from men," that there was no danger in "contemplation and profound discovery in these things,"[78] Porter insisted in his letter to Wingate that there ought not be one view of Scripture accepted by historians and another taught to children for fear of disturbing their reverence for the book[79] and set as the mark of a true return to the religion of Jesus that it be accessible to common folk.[80]

If it is true that *A Treatise Concerning Religious Affections* is Edwards' chief work, and if it is true that all that is written there is gleaned from the "record of Paul's experience,"[81] then Edwards and Porter alike, and the latter in a period when it was most uncharacteristic, found the reason and justification for their aesthetic-affectional approach in the theology of Paul. To the riddle whether the similarities between Edwards and Porter lay in the former's influence on the latter, or whether Porter's discovery of the apostle threw him back upon his New England heritage, Porter gave a clue at the midpoint of his career:

> Jonathan Edwards, who got his Christianity from Paul and John, but possessed it as his own through an experience like theirs, found this to be the natural order of the Christian life: First, a true sense of the glorious excellency of Jesus Christ; then, and therefore, the conviction of the truth and reality of God and Christ and the gospel; and finally self-dedication to God and renunciation of the world. The order is the reverse of that in which Tolstoy puts the marks of all prophecy. . . . I think that Edwards is right. . . .[82]

Toward the close of his life, Porter wrote:

> I incline then to get from Paul my theology, in the sense in which I
> have one — and it is from Paul that I get this sense.[83]

So it was Paul furnished the prior stimulus, but the influence
and support of Edwards were not the less great for all of that.

Porter's "Religion of the Spirit," which he never released
for publication — once, perhaps, a carefully threaded
whole, now only a mass of repetition, supplement and
unpaginated scraps — but which served as a kind of fount or
spring from which to draw for other works, as well as that
fondness for the term "Spirit" as encompassing everything
he had to say, links Porter as intimately with Edwards as
anything else. For both, "Spirit" constituted the sum and
substance of a life's work. For Edwards, everything hinged
on identifying beauty with the essence of the divine as Spirit:

> The Holy Ghost is Himself the delight and joyfulness of the Father
> in that idea (of Himself which He has in His Son) and of the idea in
> the Father. . . . So that, if we turn in all the ways in the world, we
> shall never be able to make more than these three, God, the idea of
> God, and delight in God.[84]

So it was in the Spirit himself that the "substantial" beauty of
God was to be found.[85]

In answer to his question, "Do we not need an approach
of the more Platonic type to the nature of spirit?"[86] — the
very same put by those Cambridge Platonists on whom
Edwards had drawn[87] — Porter replied that "Spirit"
denoted immanence, personality, moral character.[88] It
denoted something beyond a mere book religion or religion
of authority.[89] The entire history of Judaism and its issuance
in Christian faith constituted a development from
nationalism toward universalism, from ritual toward ethical
religion, from legalism toward a spiritual religion.[90] "Spirit"
characterized a "right return" to the religion of Jesus.[91]
Above all, it signalized the synthesis between the objective

and the subjective, the particular and the universal, between the Jesus of history and Jesus in Christian experience. It tokened the union between inwardness, freedom, the interpretation of Jesus by Spirit, and love, the interpretation of Spirit by Jesus.[92] And for both men, justification lay in the theology of Paul and John for whom faith consisted in a oneness between persons in knowledge and will and love,[93] a doctrine "in the most proper sense a religion of the Spirit."[94] This was also Edwards' "doctrine:"

> The God whom Edwards discovered for himself was the God whom Paul knew, the God and Father of our Lord Jesus Christ, the God of Love. The Christian religion was to him nothing but God Himself in his own person, the Divine Love, entering into human beings and making them his own.[95]

Both Edwards and Porter were willing to take another step. Edwards spoke of the spiritual as the "most substantial,"[96] a sentence which Porter revised to read, "'substance' is not greater but less than personality."[97] Edwards contended that if all the spirits in the universe were for a time deprived of consciousness and God's consciousness also intermitted, "the Universe for that time would cease to be of itself,"[98] and Porter could speak of Spirit as "the all uniting energy of all things."[99] The same charge which William Ellery Channing levelled at Edwards, viz., that by making God the only active power of the universe he had annihilated the creature, had become a "pantheist" and obliged men to ask whether such a thing as matter exists, could have been aimed at Porter as well.[100] On the surface, at least, there is little difference between affirming that the world as known exists only in the mind and stating that "it is precisely in those intuitions which transcend sense that we have the best right to believe that we come into contact with reality."[101]

Our comparison makes possible a forty-year delayed response to the censorious Bicknell[102] — Porter indeed had a theology, and its support, if not its origin, lay in large measure with Jonathan Edwards, his great-great-grandfather.

II. *Porter and Edwards Contrasted*:

For all their similarities, Edwards and Porter are still a study in contrasts. First of all, there was a difference in the matter of gifts. Porter described Edwards as "the greatest mind and spirit that we at Yale can claim,"[103] but of his own work entertained serious doubts. On a little scrap over which he had scribbled the words "On Retiring and Early Years at Yale," Porter had written that having done with lecturing, which everyone knows is "an antiquated and irrational method of teaching," he no longer had the feeling he was doing what he ought not and not doing what he ought, and then added:

> If I continue to teach by writing I am using a method that has not yet fallen under the ban. To read books is still a valid part of education. So to write a book is still admittedly a proper thing to do. For myself I think it is a dangerous undertaking. It may become a habit. It is very easy to overdo it, and *very* hard (as it seems to me) to write a book that really needs to be written. But there are advantages. No one is required to read it.[104]

What occasioned the first great contrast between the two men, however, was none of their own doing — the advent of historical critical study. The appearance of scientific, biblical research required a re-translation of the Edwardsean sense-thought question and in an idiom Porter best understood:

> When now the historical use of the Bible makes its dogmatic use impossible, what is one to do who recognizes that the Bible has religious power in itself apart from the historical facts and independent of their recovery?[105]

The question, Porter said, was rendered most acute when made to read concerning the relation between Jesus in history and Jesus in the mind of the Christian,[106] between the Jesus whose earthly life and teachings, death and resurrection made such great changes in human spiritual history, and the Christ whose spiritual indwelling changes men into his image.[107] The antimony was represented, not now by the views of Locke and Hume, but again, by the History of Religions School and the liberal schools on the Continent, the one attempting to demonstrate that the Gospels contain something which can be accepted as certain fact, the other maintaining that Christianity does not consist in the acceptance of an historical datum but of an ideal or principle.[108]

Porter clearly asserted the right of historical critical research and treated the Gospels as historical documents as more or less records of fact. Such research, Porter believed, contributed to the religious experience,[109] might even lead the researcher to the "religion of Jesus"[110] and free him of that overlay of superstition and dogma so unpalatable to the modern mind.[111] For Porter, the History of Religions School appeared as principal protector of the right to criticism, and he freely used its comparative method, as, e.g., in his psychological interpretation of Jesus' exorcisms, a tactic familiar to the *Religionsgeschichtler* since the days of Wilhelm Bousset.

It is just as obvious, however, that Porter was at odds with that school, not merely for its vaunted optimism over the results of its criticism or its tacit assumption that the better historian was the better Christian. Something else lay at the root of his attack upon Ritschl and Harnack and their American counterpart McGiffert, or of his curious tendency to daub Martin Kähler and his old friend Bacon with the same brush and to prescribe Wilhelm Hermann, but above all, Ernst Troeltsch — that bulwark against historicism — as an antidote.[112] That something else constituted a commitment, a pledge to ideas or notions which led Porter to a drastic revision of his Edwardsean heritage.

First of all, Porter was committed to Christianity as an ideal. With all his willingness, on occasion at least, to be classed with Ritschl or Harnack,[113] he viewed Christianity as "a certain truth and ideal."[114] And that ideal took its shape less from Locke, Hume, the English Puritans or Edwards than from Lessing, Kant or the Romanticists. Porter put it clearly enough in his lectures on New Testament Biblical Theology:

> Christianity is not only definition and dogma, it is an ideal, a problem, first in the believer, then in the world at large. . . . Kant, after denying the validity of the arguments for God, posits the spiritual and moral nature of man, and hence finds God as the ideal. There is something akin to this in Christianity — acceptance of Christ as Lord and the Divine Ideal.[115]

Theology's task, then, was not to concentrate upon a particular action of God nor to exclude Jesus from that "development" which the historian must trace,[116] but rather to distinguish the Idea, that "eternal truth beneath the accidents and incidents of human life and thought."[117] Such statements, coupled with a description of history as "the history of the divine instruction and guidance of men,"[118] of the history of religions as the history of the "mysterious coming and going of the spirit, amid the progressive movements of national and intellectual life,"[119] an instruction discernible in a "community of men bound together and working together in righteousness,"[120] are strikingly reminiscent of the thought of G. E. Lessing and all his company.

Why, then, the "return to Jesus" or to his religion, if not to establish some historical datum on which faith might rest? For Porter, the answer was simple enough: the idea, the eternal verity is symbolized in persons, and inasmuch as "Spirit" had its supreme manifestation in Jesus, return to him, to his "genius" and personality unlocked its secrets. If, as Arnold had written, the personality of Jesus was "the revelation of the Eternal, not ourselves, which makes for righteousness,"[121] then the explanation to Christianity was to be found in that personality, a contention reinforced by Richard Reitzenstein, cited by Porter as often as any other continental.[122] The Gospels gave that personality clarity and harmony. Paul's religion was wholly controlled by it. Schweitzer had missed the truth of it all and substituted apocalyptic fancy in Jesus and Paul for personality.[123] Thus, historical criticism, conceived as the pursuit of personality, made possible an arrival into "the living presence of great persons" — the only means to truer discipleship and a higher religious life.[124] The idea was as old as the Romanticists, Goethe and Fichte: personality was the bridge to actualization. The idea, the ideal which should determine human life, achieved its incorporation in the genius. With Porter, the beauty of excellence of Edwards' thought had lost its ontological status and come to be identified with character.

Horace Bushnell, through whom "Coleridge Romanticism" may have penetrated American theology, had contended for a "Divine Logos" in the world which arranged the forms of things so as to typify what was in men's souls and disposed the relations between those things so as to be reflected in language.[125] But because words, terms and all such were never exact, being only, as Bushnell called them, "names of genera,"[126] it followed that no single proposition and hence no fixed form of dogma was capable of giving form to the whole truth. For that reason, a change or even a multiplication of forms was required for the truth's apprehension.[127] The Bible itself shared all the inadequacies of language. Yet, because it furnished a plethora of forms and figures it could yield the single vision once those forms were all embraced. In a lyrical mood Bushnell wrote:

> But whosoever wants . . . really to behold and receive all truth, and would have the truth-world overhang him as an impyrean of stars, complex, multitudinous, striving antagonistically, yet comprehended, height above height, and deep under deep, in a boundless score of harmony; what man soever, content with no small rote of logic and catechism, reaches with true hunger after this, and will offer himself to the many-sided forms of the Scripture with a perfectly ingenuous and receptive spirit; he shall find his nature flooded with senses, vastnesses, and powers of truth, such as it is even greatness to feel.[128]

Given the inability of the single symbol as creed to reflect the entire truth, it was a small thing for Porter to draw the conclusion that Jesus as symbol must himself be subordinate to the "ideal." Edwards perhaps evoked the thought, but Romanticism its interpretation. Porter wrote that "Edwards, who was not a liberal theologian, declared that Jesus felt a difference between himself and God,"[129] and,

> Coleridge was wholly right in his contention that no special article of faith containing a doctrine of the Bible should be added to those faiths which constitute the Christian religion. . . . Something very like this I should for my part want to say also of Jesus himself.[130]

In as unguarded a moment as he ever enjoyed, Porter made clear where he stood:

> Let us suppose that Jesus never lived or that the picture of him in the gospels is so far an idealization that the historical Jesus is hidden from us, would it follow that the ideal is untrue? This is really the crucial question. . . . To me it seems that our Christian experience justifies us only in saying that it comes to us as truth and works in us as a saving and renewing power, through the gospel picture of Jesus Christ; not that the truth of the picture depends upon its historical actuality. . . . We assent to the truth, and would assent to it no less if the picture were proved fiction and not fact, and would I hope be wise enough to treasure the gospels no less if we were led to regard them not as poetic truth embodied in actual historical fact, but as poetic truth embodied in imagined historical form.[131]

It was because Ritschlianism, McGiffert, the Niebuhrs and friend Bacon could not let the symbol go, could not identify the historical Jesus with the "idea,"[132] in a word, could not meet Aristotle's test of universality,[133] that they all came under Porter's ban.

One need not, of course, go to extremes. If for Porter the Ritschlians were the Scylla of an extreme particularity, the liberals were the Charybdis of an extreme universality. For the sake of the idea's universality, Porter was compelled to retain particularity at some point. Without an adequate symbol, how could that universality be recognized? The prophets, then, had to be spared a certain uniqueness. They were without analogy within the religious history of the ancient orient, not merely because they opposed a spiritualized religiosity to priestly, cultic religion, but because they preached universality. A certain uniqueness lay with the wisdom literature as well, that "surprising element" in Judaism which reflected Israel's capacity for a religion of nature and humanity in addition to a supernatural and national religion of law. And it was from prophetism and Wisdom, not from law and apocalyptic, that Jesus and Paul drew their strength.

Still and all, the accent, the emphasis lay on the universal, and with it the natural. If Edwards had argued that the religious affections, however adequate to man's natural craving, were a "gift," that those "gracious influences which the saints are subjects of" were "entirely above nature, altogether of a different kind from any thing that men find within themselves by nature,"[134] for Porter such a "new spiritual sense" as Edwards had in mind was available to man as such. Porter had some acquaintance with the Neo-orthodoxy just being introduced to the United States, and which was later to consign him and a host of others like him to oblivion. How well he was acquainted with it is difficult to tell. He had read Bultmann's *Jesus* in English translation, and something of Barth. His references to the two men were infrequent and reflect only an understanding of their similarities, nothing of their differences. But whatever Porter had read of them he did not like, because he thought they lacked a truly "natural" theology, that is, they denied that universal, "humanistic character" of Jesus' thought and of all true religion. Barth and his confreres were thus described as trying to force theology off from sympathy with a belief in every way in which man seeks God, and Bultmann fell under the same judgment:

> I don't see how Bultmann (or any one) can escape knowing what God requires of man by knowing directly, i.e. from within, by what in his own nature and in the ideals and purposes of men, what is excellent, and what . . . is much more in God than in man. But is known as in God, because it is in man and man knows it to be good.[135]

The second great contrast between Porter and Edwards lay in Porter's drastic revision of Edwards' synthesis. Both agreed that sense and thought or history and faith needed uniting. Both agreed that the unity was to be achieved in terms of the aesthetic. But what Porter meant by "aesthetic" or "affectional" was a far cry from Edwards' view. For his definition of these terms and his consequent view of the synthesis, Porter drew from another spring. He drew from Longinus, first of all, that unidentifiable Greek who for two hundred years had furnished grist for the mill of every English and French romantic who believed that feeling, emotion and subjectivity were more valid than all the rules of art.[136] He drew from Coleridge and Wordsworth in whom that ancient rhetorician reached his apogee; from Robert Lowth and Arnold and Bushnell — all of them in the direct line of Longinian succession. They had all told what kind of mood the Bible and true religion required — "wonder and transport," said Longinus; "feeling," said Coleridge; "passion," said Wordsworth, and Bishop Lowth had defended Scripture against its attackers by identifying the poetic and the religious.[137] Arnold spoke of "enjoyment," of Jesus' "restoration of the intuition" and his "method of inwardness;"[138] Bushnell reiterated Lowth's alliance of religion and poetry, and spoke of symbols as requiring "insight."[139] What was left to Porter was a mere restatement: the New Testament, Jesus, Paul and John enunciated what only "wonder and transport," "inwardness," "insight," "passion," feeling and subjectivity could grasp.

Edwards was no romanticist. If he knew of the Longinian tradition, he had no appetite for it.[140] His battles over the Great Awakening led him meticulously to distinguish between spurious and true conversions, and thus to assign far more of the rational and volitional to the affective or emotional than Porter or the Romanticists would allow.[141] He struggled to unite both aspects into a beauty aimed at by both mind and heart[142] and aimed at giving that beauty objective, structural and ontological status.[143] Edwards, in other words, attempted a definition of the aesthetic which embraced the total man,[144] a definition which allowed no distinction between spirit and matter.[145] But what Edwards had joined together Porter had put asunder, either because he understood Edwards in terms of a naïve contrast between head and heart,[146] or because he had made that prior commitment to the idea as universal, as "natural," had made that pledge to the "humanistic" which left no room for the idea of the "sense" of the divine beauty as gift.

At any rate, given his definition of the aesthetic, Porter conceived his task as separating the imaginative truth expressed in the language of feeling from its occasion in historical fact.[147] To the extent Bushnell could call those poetic forms or symbols mere "husks" to be stripped away from the "pure truths of thought presented in them,"[148] he retained whatever orthodoxy clung to a nineteenth century Christocentric liberal. Porter, on the other hand, tended to identify the idea with the form itself, to subordinate the historical occasion to it, and proved himself the more genuine romantic:

> While we may by historical criticism remove the form . . . to discover the reality which the form has often concealed, yet in the end the higher reality is to be felt in the form itself rather than sought behind it.[149]

The stories of Jesus' birth, the nature miracles and references to the physical aspects of the appearance of the risen Christ — all these required the "unembarrassed application of standards of literature," that is, were to be construed in a "poetic sense." Paul's "ingenious arguments" concerning the end of the law, above all the Christologies in Romans 8, I Corinthians 8, Philippians 2 and Colossians 1, were not literally but poetically true, true as imagic, true as the language of "lofty emotion." And, they were reproducible. If, as Lowth had said, poetry was imitation, and the most agreeable of all imitations was that of emotion,[150] then that moral effort which Porter demanded as the "chief test" of a truly religious life was an imitation achieved through the appreciation of forms. Longinus' insistence that the great poet is the good man, or Bushnell's word that the "real

amount of true theology" depended on the "more cultivated
and nicer apprehension of symbol,"[151] bore riper fruit in
Porter. He could wax rhapsodic on Christ's death and
resurrection as typical of the moral task of all men;[152] on
men's becoming "altogether what Jesus was" and on the
Christian's imitation of God,[153] but his *imitatio* seemed to
derive from an inspiration conjured up by the form
itself — by those stories, narratives and utterances which
needed to be read and reread through "tact and insight."

Naturally, there were exceptions. When Porter came
against the apocalyptic utterances of the New Testament, he
could treat them in the style of his contemporaries and
winnow out from such "forms" their genuine "substance" in
the idea that the conquest of evil and genuine rulership
belong to Christ and those who are his.[154] He could oppose
to such forms still others which deserved the greater
concentration,[155] or he could dismiss them out of hand:

> In regard to the accounts of first and last things . . . we need
> nothing but an historical account and explanation, and by this are
> freed from any further responsibility.[156]

Porter could also insist that forms which appeared to be
eschatological or apocalyptic in reality were not; that Paul
himself had prepared for their "weakening" and that such
interpretations as Schweitzer's were a "mistake," resulting
from too great anxiety over modernizing the New
Testament.[157] Yet, Porter's greatest objection to the
eschatological lay in his belief that its fixing a future and
outward goal betrayed the moral and inward quality of
Jesus' teaching which aimed at producing in men a faith such
as his, a faith opposed to exclusivism, externality and
intervention. This was the entire burden of Porter's
interpretation of the temptations and Lord's Prayer.[158] In
other words, since the *imitatio* somehow hinged on the form,
and since the form of the eschatological/apocalyptic
inhibited reproduction or imitation, it needed to be
reinterpreted, if not relegated to the category of what

Matthew Arnold had once called "extra-belief" or *Aberglaube*.[159]

Porter's revision of Edwards' aesthetic view and his consequent notion of the scholar's task open a gulf between these two New Englanders wide enough to discourage attempts to trace their continuity. For, once that romantic urge in Porter is noted, it is easy to conclude that the similarities earlier marked are only superficial. Define the synthesis in terms of feeling and emotion as such, and the antinomy to be reconciled immediately takes on another shape. Now it is not the antinomy of history and faith — it is the antinomy of the world as sensed and perceived and another, suprasensible world.

The plain fact of the matter is that Porter could not live with the world he saw, a mechanistic world of necessity in which cause reigned supreme. He had to introduce a world "wholly apart from nature,"[160] a "something which lies deeper," a "greater thing" which it was the business of historical criticism to uncover, and with which the sensible, perceivable world had to be united. And the union lay elsewhere than in the world Porter saw. Edwards remained a predestinarian because of his "vision of the inviolable sequence of things," because of his assurance that "throughout the universe, and into the utmost fastnesses of the Godhead, cause perpetually reigns,"[161] a necessity which to his mind was not at all inconsistent with true liberty, and hence with praise or blame. Edwards accused his enemies of abandoning the world and thus of traducing liberty by introducing a notion of it as "consisting in the Will's first acting, and so causing its own acts; and determining, and so causing its own determinations; or choosing, and so causing its own choice."[162] The Arminians, wrote Edwards, had thus deserted things as they are and reduced men to automata by tricking them into believing they had willed themselves.[163] Porter's response to the Pauline idea of predestination was typical of the reaction of Edwards' contemporaries:

> [Paul's] conception of predestination is perhaps the worst of all
> from our point of view because it seems a denial of the very thing

that Paul saw in God in the face of Christ, that is love. It seems
arbitrary. It seems cruel. It cannot be made to look otherwise. It
does not seem fatherly. So we are in a region where we are not
going to follow Paul unless we want to.[164]

Porter clearly did not want to, not because the "sublime," the
grandeur or horror of natural objects was too much for him
and he needed some Kantian, suprasensible idea of Nature to
embrace it all. For Porter there was no sublimity at all in
sheer, naked causality.

Porter, then, actually had tongue in cheek when he talked
of the "natural." It was the ideal, the supernatural reality
which was natural. And that long train of Romanticists on
whom he came to depend saw it just as he did. Neither
Coleridge nor Wordsworth dealt with the natural world. For
both, the natural was always the ideal. Coleridge was
offended by the naturalistic implications of, for example,
Edmund Burke's aesthetic theory, and Wordsworth had no
stomach for the "picturesque." Indeed, the tyranny of the
natural eye had to be broken before a man could really see.[165]
And though Porter noted a "certain unadjusted dualism" in
Coleridge, he agreed:

> [Coleridge's] part was to write poems in which the incidents and
> agents were to be in part supernatural . . . Wordsworth . . . was to
> take subjects from ordinary life . . . and to excite a feeling
> analogous to the supernatural by awakening the mind's attention
> to . . . the loveliness and the wonders of the world before us.[166]

When he wrote that the poetic truth should always get "the
higher right and value" over the historical fact, the antinomy
remained the same. Only the names were changed to protect
the innocent. Porter always broke the tie between the
"supernatural" and "the world before us" in favor of the
former as idea, verity, value.

In his student years, Porter had read Lotze in the classes
of the "animist" George T. Ladd. His reference to that
sentence in Lotze's *Microcosmos* as a "proclamation of
emancipation," deserving a place in any account of his

mental history,[167] gives the clue to the fact that for him that
other world, "wholly apart," had its home in the self. Lotze,
as any reliable introduction to philosophy will tell, knew the
modern-mechanistic view of nature from the ground up, but
refused to conceive the world in any other fashion than as a
function of the conscious subject. Reality was not the stuff
but rather the *effect* of consciousness and the external world
needed to be interpreted in terms of mind, the only knowable
entity. For Lotze, the entire universe was nothing but a
complex of immaterial essences, analogous to the variety,
change and development in the human soul, and underneath
it all, guaranteeing unity to that variety and persistence to
that   change   and   development   there   lay   "Spirit,"
"personality," the great *Weltgrund* in which everything
spiritual and corporeal originated.[168] In Lotze Porter found
sophisticated support for his romanticism. Armed with a
"soul theory" or a "teleological idealism," Porter could allow
the world of inviolable sequence to run its course, confident
with Coleridge, Wordsworth and all the rest that the really
real lay elsewhere:

> Wordsworth has his rights in the interpretation of nature by the
> side of Darwin. . . . The universe is one, and in it everything has its
> place and so far its explanation. But . . . the supreme values in the
> universe do not lie in the mechanism. . . . The mechanism of the
> world runs on whether we recognize it or not. . . . But of the
> spiritual values of nature we cannot be so sure that they exist apart
> from us. . . . It is precisely in those intuitions which transcend
> sense that we have the best right to believe that we come into
> contact with reality.[169]

If the home of reality is the self, the inner life — that
entity of "essential and supreme worth";[170] if the Kingdom of
God is "within you" as Wellhausen and Arnold had said,[171]
indeed, "within human nature or nowhere"; then the self in
some way furnishes the criterion of what is true and what is
false, what is great and what less great. Then it is "whatever
finds me" in the New Testament, as Coleridge and Bushnell
after him had put it,[172] "that constitutes my religion," then
the true test of thinking about Christ is that it be "according

to the Christian." David Hume, perhaps, had aided and abetted many a romantic by discarding the old notion of beauty as residing in its object, by his preoccupation with the experience of the mind perceiving the object, but there was more, or, there was less to Hume than to Kant who found beauty and the sublime in the perceiving subject, and it was that more or less which led Edwards to reinterpret human understanding to include sensibility. Without such reinterpretation, Edwards could have made no cognitive claim about God himself. He could only have affirmed that the self was all. Now, Porter came close to such an affirmation when in answer to Benjamin Bacon's interpretation of the cross as once for all he wrote "No! Paul makes the Christian repeat the redemptive deed of God," and then added, "really, our self is Christ."[173] The "transcendence" of Edwards, carved out of a "sense" for what had been expressed in the world, and which he could put in traditional fashion as well as in any other,[174] had come a'cropper on Porter's romantic self. Shirley Jackson Case, Porter's one-time pupil and as immanentalist a theologian as ever drew breath, knew enough to see the consequences. After outlining to his old teacher and mentor a series of proposed lectures on the evolutionary conception of Christianity, he concluded:

> I contend, that the evolutionary conception of religion while it eliminates supernaturalism does not eliminate God. . . . If I may repeat one of your phrases, we are not only "in the stream of Christianity," we *are* the stream.[175]

There may have been times when Porter was aware of this solipsism in his thought. He had noted that under Josiah Royce's touch God and Christ appeared to dissolve into the "beloved community," though his principle objection to Royce's view was that it assigned more concreteness to the community than to the individual, and, as Porter confessed, "I am very much of an individualist."[176] He had detected Wilhelm Herrmann's penchant for converting certainties as to truth into certainties as to fact, though he added that if

Jesus had not lived or acted as reported, the life he is described as living would still be good.[177] He had stated that the metaphysical, literal, physical and strictly supernatural could not be excluded from Paul, though he believed it was to Paul but a means to an end.[178] Aware of solipsism or not, in the end Porter could protect himself from its threat simply by allowing for "two religions," "two Christianities" in the New Testament, the religion *about* and the religion *of* Jesus.[179] But he reserved the latter for himself and left others to their own choices.

Confine the universal to the perceiving subject, make the self the mirror of the idea, more, give truth a home in the self and nowhere else and it is almost certain that the single self will have but a single vision. That was true of Porter. He searched for that *unio mystica* of all the separated functions and concepts of human thought, of theology. Though he never released his "Religion of the Spirit," everything he thought and did belongs under that rubric. It was "Spirit" tokened the rational versus the dogmatic; "Spirit" marked the inward versus the supernatural or external — "Spirit" sought in "thoroughly immanent fashion," i.e. in the self. It was "Spirit" denoted the ethical and typical, the universal, the *imitatio* versus the eschatological and exclusivistic. "Spirit" singled out the prophetic from the priestly, the "poetic truth" from the historical fact or fancy. "Spirit" summed up the religion of Paul — the "key" to Jesus — and by "Spirit" men were most joined to the one from whom they seemed most to be separated — "Spirit," one and indivisible. Porter enjoyed huge precedent for his single vision. It was there in Wordsworth:

> I have felt A presence that disturbs me with the joy Of elevated thoughts; a sense sublime Of something. . . . Whose dwelling is the light of setting suns, And the round ocean, and the living air, And the blue sky, and in the mind of man: A motion and a spirit, that impels All thinking things, all objects of all thought, And rolls through all things.[180]

"Spirit," or "personality" had been the *Weltgrund*, the

unifying, universal substance for Lotze. In that unitary, undivided "Spirit" everything originated, material and immaterial. Nor was Bushnell one to disallow the mystic's single vision:

> The very last thing to be feared is, that . . . the stern, iron-limbed speculative logic of our New England theology, will receive some fatal damage from a trace of the mystic element. It will produce no overturnings, sap no foundations. . . . It will enter only as life came into the bones; which, though they rose up into a limbered and active state, and were hidden somewhat from the eye, by an envelop of muscle and skin, were yet as good bones as before; probably as much better and more systematic, as there was more of the life-order in them and about them.[181]

The simplicity, the common, the uncomplicated about which Porter loved to speak and write — it all served that single vision. The parables of Jesus were simple and did not require interpretation, because, in Arnold's words, faith was the "recognition of what is perfectly clear,"[182] and what was clear was that "our self is Christ." It was a long journey from Edwards who spurned nondifferentiation, demanded plurality in God himself and wrote that "in a being that is absolutely without any plurality there cannot be excellency, for there can be no such thing as consent or agreement."[183]

Finally, beneath or above it all there lay Porter's "secret religion," spawned by the Idea and nursed by the time — his confidence in development, in progress, in the idea's power to prevail. Whereas Edwards denied there ever would be a moment when justice would be done, Porter agreed with Graf Hermann Keyserling (1881-1946) who had reduced every religion to a single truth to be grasped through "meditation," that "Christianity is actively believing that evils can be overcome,"[184] that man's highest calling was to cooperate with the "cosmic spirit" in the effort to make good prevail.[185] Porter believed the processes of nature, interpreted as the Kingdom-idea, presented to men the aspect of a struggle to overcome chaos and create a world of order and rationality,[186] and was confident the universe would answer to men's "highest efforts" and "most earnest endeavor."[187] He dubbed the League of Nations a concrete expression of that hope of universality, inwardness and good will inspiring the nations, the silver lining in the cloud of the First World War:

> The world war . . . has made mankind more conscious of its ideal of community and fellowship, and seems to be carrying us faster toward the realization of human brotherhood than peace and prosperity were doing.[188]

Faith in the freedom of God's children as inseparably linked with popular sovereignty, belief in the Kingdom of God as the inevitable betterment of society's moral condition belonged to that amalgam of American civil religion of which Porter was a sophisticated representative. He agreed that one thing which distinguished his age from earliest Christianity was the idea of evil as "incidental and remediable."[189] Santayana's portrait of that happy American who "thinks life splendid and blameless, without stopping to consider how far folly and malice may be inherent in it,"[190] could have been sat for by Porter. His private life may have been a different story, but of that we've no license to tell. His thought, his theology, had room for the romantic, the idealistic, the heroic, and there was little of the tragic in it.

In the earliest pieces of Reinhold Niebuhr, the most famous of Porter's students, the traces of his old professor's scheme are as clear as crystal. Niebuhr, just as Porter, rhapsodized on the "ideal"[191] and Jesus as its incarnation,[192] as giving historical reality to the "Christ idea."[193] He could even call Jesus the "God of the ideal."[194] Niebuhr also agreed that the "religious rhetorician" must take his standards from the artist, the poet,[195] and like Porter tried to "discover the glimpses of the eternal in the common scene."[196] He wrote that the final test of any religion was its ability to prompt ethical action on the basis of "reverence for personality,"[197] and shouldered Porter's prejudice against the priestly — "the priest," wrote Niebuhr, "is more numerous

than the prophet because human selfishness is as
determining in religion as in other fields."[198] And, Niebuhr's
attack on magic as an "enemy of morality" was nothing but a
retranslation of Porter's aversion to the sacramental. Nor
were the heroics of Porter's ethic lost to Niebuhr. He could
refer to "prizes of the spirit which can be won only by heroic
effort"[199] and appealed to a mutual friend, Matthew Arnold,
for support:

> Charge once more then and be dumb, Let the victors when they
> come, When the forts of folly fall, Find thy body by the wall.[200]

These are but random samplings. It would require a proper
systematician to find in his first attempts or in all of
Niebuhr's work corroboration for his own testimony to
Porter's influence:

> I completed my graduate training at the Divinity School of Yale
> University. . . . Professor Porter was at that time the New
> Testament theologian. His lucid and comprehensive exposition of
> New Testament theology made a tremendous impression, and the
> notes I took in his classes are the only school notes I still
> preserve.[201]

As yet, no appraisal of Niebuhr's thought has ever bothered
with Frank Chamberlain Porter.

But, as every student of Niebuhr knows, there was
something about Porter's type of religion which stuck in the
young Detroiter's craw. The romanticism of his school days
ill equipped him for later battle with the Baalim of Ford or
General Motors. It appeared a deception, a betrayal of
religion to sentimental optimism.[202] Its belief that human
history was the last chapter in the beautiful story of progress
had become a facade behind which lurked the "brutal facts of
modern industrial civilization."[203] It was a compromise with
the status quo which relaxed moral restraint on social
institutions and led to quietism in respect of social ills.[204]
Such a single vision, such a "monism" as Porter's which had

relegated apocalyptic to limbo failed to gauge the measure of resistance its ideal had to meet.[205] It needed to have its fears aroused with the picture of the tempting serpent in Genesis, Niebuhr continued, or with the moral realism of a Thomas Huxley.[206] It had to come to grips with the reality of God and evil,[207] with the sinfulness of the creative process in the world and nature, with the truth that the moral values dignifying a man's life were "embattled in his own soul."[208] It needed to settle with brutalities which were most real where they were most covert — in the lives of the "respectable classes."[209] In his "open" diary, Niebuhr penned an early entry which, while still trailing loyalty to "idea" and "symbol," summed up his discontent and omened a stance for which he later became a household word:

> We had a communion service tonight . . . and I preached on the text "We preach Christ crucified". . . . It was only a few years ago that I did not know what to make of the cross; at least I made no more of it than to recognize it as a historic fact which proved the necessity of paying a high price for our ideals. Now I see it as a symbol of ultimate reality. . . . It is because the cross of Christ symbolizes something in the very heart of reality, something in universal experience that it has its central place in history.[210]

Years later, on the occasion of the Munich betrayal, Niebuhr reminisced over the fracture of his romanticism, affirmed the right of the "New Orthodoxy," yet pledged an old allegiance to something he had learned from Porter:

> [Jesus] is . . . the source of my despair. Only in that despair and in repentance can he become the source of a new hope. This . . . emphasis is true enough. Only it will tempt us "to continue in sin that grace may abound" if we do not preserve what is genuinely Christian in liberal Christian moralism: the insistence that Christ is our law, our ideal, our norm, and the revelation of our essential being.[211]

In Hermann Hesse's *Glasperlenspiel*, the Benedictine Pater Jakobus thunders at Josef Knecht's attempt to comprehend everything under the sun in a single rhythm or formula:

> You treat world history as a mathematician treats mathematics, where there are only laws and formulas, but no reality, no good and evil, no time, no yesterday, no tomorrow, only an eternal, shallow mathematical present. . . . Whoever looks at history, should . . . have respect for the incomprehensible truth, reality and particularity of occurrence. Doing history, dear fellow, is no joke or irresponsible game. It assumes a man is aware he is after the impossible yet necessary and all-important. It means abandoning oneself to chaos while still believing in order and meaning. It is a very sober task, young man, and perhaps a tragic one.[212]

Once the Edwardsean stimulus and the romanticist revision behind Porter's thought are recognized, it becomes a marvel of consistency. There is a singleness to it which makes the work of his more celebrated colleague, Benjamin Bacon, fitful by comparison. But what gave to Porter's thought its coherence renders it liable to the same criticism as the glass bead player's game. The preoccupation with "Spirit," with the all-encompassing idea to which its very symbol, human and divine, was subordinated; that stern refusal to see the world about him as it was, full of the contingent, spontaneous, and irrational; to see it only in light of the idea, and the relegating of historical criticism to the level of a mere tool for the idea's beholding; finally, that centering of the idea in the single self, so that externality or the other became a mere projection of it — all that made Frank Chamberlain Porter's theology an a-temporal, a-historical thing.

Porter, of course, was forgotten. Due to the strange, new continental import, a wave of oblivion swept over him the day he retired.[213] And if his portrait still hangs alongside the fireplace in the Common Room of the Divinity School, green students and professors filing past it on their way to lunch are still asking what possible connection that bald little fellow with the celluloid collar and string tie had with Yale. Porter should not be forgotten. He was among the first to uncover the place of apocalyptic in Judaism. He was the very first of his generation to wrestle with the hermeneutical question, the question of the "etiquette" of the Bible's interpretation. His sight of Jesus through the eyes of Paul set him against the whole stream of his time. And, no less important, he should not have been forgotten because he was a type of an American theology still in vogue though, perhaps, wearing tarnish, a type urging the use of language and thought forms belonging to systems born in the idealisms of Britain and the Continent. He was representative of those who abandon a heritage as typically American as such can ever be and help to drive further that wedge between theology and philosophy in this country. Single, indivisible Being and the exaltation of the poet's ability to "descry" it, the consequent call to return to the language *of* Jesus if not to his religion, the solipsism which reduces God to an event occurring in the midst of affirming one's own and the other's existence — a capacity for which the self already comes equipped; refusal to come to grips with a world and nature which threaten to render the ancient notion that the self has any inherent identity or that all is somehow given with it an impossibility — it was all there in Porter, home grown. The newer form of his game might have been less frenzied had Porter's domesticated variety been studied and examined. But, as Goethe once said in a moment of eloquent pique: "the idiots all want to begin at the beginning, independently . . . without help."

1. R. H. Charles, *Studies in the Apocalypse* (Edinburgh: T. & T. Clark, 1915), pp. 72-76; John D. Davis, Review of *The Messages of the Apocalyptical Writers* in *The Princeton Theological Review*, IV, 3 (July, 1906), p. 408.

2. W. D. Davies, *Paul and Rabbinic Judaism* (London: SPCK, 1948), p. 151. In a review of *The Mind of Christ in Paul*, a certain E. J. Bicknell referred to Porter's "rejection of all metaphysical thinking," and to his "inveterate hostility" to a theological interpretation of the person of Christ, a stance which that reviewer dubbed as "strangely old-fashioned." Cf. *Theology, A Monthly Journal of Historic Christianity*, XXIII (July-December, 1931), p. 111.

3. J. E. Frame, Review of *The Mind of Christ in Paul* in *Union Theological Seminary Alumni Bulletin* (1931), p. 85.

4. Burton Scott Easton, Review of *The Mind of Christ in Paul*, pp. 207ff.

5. Morton Scott Enslin, "A Study of Paul That Is Different," *The Journal of Religion*, XI, 4 (October, 1931), p. 620.

6. Harold R. Willoughby, Review of *The Mind of Christ in Paul*, *Religious Education* XXVI, 4 (April, 1931), p. 371f.

7. Letter from Erwin R. Goodenough, New Haven, Connecticut, March 8, 1937. Porter's colleague, Benjamin Bacon, stated that if his own study of the "new legalism" of Matthew lent confirmation to Porter's contention that Jesus and Paul were essentially at one in their revolt against the tendency of Judaism to become a "religion of the book," this alone would suffice to justify its publication. Benjamin W. Bacon, "Jesus and the Law," A Study of the First 'Book' of Matthew, *Journal of Biblical Literature*, XLVII, 3/4 (1928), p. 231.

8. Henry Nelson Wieman and Bernard Eugene Meland, *American Philosophies of Religion* (Chicago: Willet, Clark & Co., 1936), pp. 44, 102, 115, 118, 127, 134f., 149, 157f., 159, 167, 179, 205.

9. The essence of the portrait appears in Roland H. Bainton, *Yale and the Ministry, op. cit.* pp. 219ff.

10. Letter of H. Richard Niebuhr (New Haven: n.d.).

11. "Religious Fellowship, Its Basis, Bounds, and Bane," *op. cit.*, p. 20.

12. Cf. "Lenten Discussion Club," *Saturday Chronicle* (March 9, 1918).

13. *The Mind of Christ in Paul, op. cit.*, p. 48.

14. Cf. Perry Miller, *Jonathan Edwards* (New York: Meridian Books, Inc., 1959), pp. 98, 112, 117, 149, 180, and Roland Andre Delattre, *Beauty and Sensibility in the Thought of Jonathan Edwards* (New Haven: Yale University Press, 1968).

15. "The Religious and the Historical Uses of the Bible," *op. cit.*, p. 251.

16. *The Mind of Christ in Paul, op. cit.*, p. 85.

17. "Religious Fellowship, Its Basis, Bounds, and Bane," *op. cit.*, p. 19f.

18. Quoted in Delattre, *op. cit.*, p. 73; cf. Miller, *op. cit.*, p. 33, and Jonathan Edwards, *Religious Affections*, ed. by John E. Smith (New Haven: Yale University Press, 1959), p. 45f.

19. "The Spirit of Christianity and the Jesus of History," *op. cit.*, p. 13.

20. Jonathan Edwards, "Religious Affections," *Jonathan Edwards, Representative Selections, With Introduction, Bibliography, And Notes*, by Clarence H. Faust and Thomas H. Johnson (New York: Hill and Wang, 1968), p. 215; cf. Jonathan Edwards, "True Grace Distinguished from the Experience of Devils," *Select Sermons of Jonathan Edwards* (London: Religious Tract Society, 1839), pp. 331, 336, 339; cf. Delattre, *op., cit.*, p. 129.
21. "Princeton Theology," *op. cit.*, p. 133.
22. "Dr. Timothy Dwight as a New Testament Scholar," *op. cit.*, p. 2.
23. Cf. Smith, *op. cit.*, p. 50, and Delattre, *op. cit.*, p. 91.
24. "The Intellectual Value of Theological Training," *op. cit.*, p. 13; "Some Recent Critical Studies in the Life of Christ," *op. cit.*, p. 1.
25. Jonathan Edwards, "True Grace Distinguished from the Experience of Devils," *op. cit.*, p. 308.
26. "The Religion of Jesus," unpublished (n.d.), p. 14.
27. From an untitled piece on things greater and less in the New Testament, *op. cit.*, p. 16.
28. Jonathan Edwards, "Religious Affections," *op. cit.*, pp. 213, 223, 252; "True Grace Distinguished from the Experience of Devils," *op. cit.*, p. 355; Delattre, *op. cit.*, p. 73.
29. Cf. Smith, *op. cit.*, pp. 29, 32.
30. Cf. *ibid.*, pp. 29, 32, 38, and Delattre, *op. cit.*, pp. 105, 112, 197.
31. *The Mind of Christ in Paul, op. cit.*, p. 160.
32. "The Place of the Sacred Book in the Christian Religion," *op. cit.*, p. 264; "Historic Facts and Religious Values in the Old Testament," *op. cit.*, p. 10; "Historic Fact and Poetic Truth in the Old Testament," *op. cit.*, pp. 8, 34; "Religion Of The Spirit," *op. cit.*, pp. 36, 40.
33. Jonathan Edwards, "Religious Affections," *op. cit.*, p. 224.
34. Smith, *op. cit.*, p. 6.
35. Roland H. Bainton, "Frank Chamberlain Porter," unpublished (n.d.), p. 2.
36. "Ought a Minister to Know Hebrew?" *op. cit.*, p. 633; Shorthand notes on the works of Benjamin W. Bacon.
37. Cf. Delattre, *op. cit.*, pp. 48, 63, n. 5, 67, 108. Cf. also the quotation on p. 125f.: "'Tis only by the discovery of the beauty of the moral perfection of Christ, that the believer is let into the knowledge of the excellency of his person, so as to know anything more of it than the devils do: and 'tis only by the knowledge of the excellency of Christ's person, that any know his sufficiency as a mediator." In "True Grace Distinguished from the Experience of Devils," Edwards had written of a "saving belief of the gospel   arising from a view of the Divine glory or beauty of the things it exhibits," *op. cit.*, pp. 357.
38. Cf. Miller, *op. cit.*, p. 95, and Delattre, *op. cit.*, pp. 8, 68f.
39. Jonathan Edwards, "The Nature of True Virtue," Faust and Johnson, *op. cit.*, p. 349.
40. "Things Greater and Less in the Bible," *op. cit.*, p. 121.

41. *New Testament Theology, op. cit.*, p. 129.
42. "The Place of the New Testament in the Christian Religion," *op. cit.*, p. 21f.
43. "Historical Facts and Religious Values in the Old Testament," *op. cit.*, p. 15.
44. "The Sufficiency of the Religion of Jesus," unpublished (n.d.), p. 80.
45. Smith, *op. cit.*, pp. 7, n. 6, 37, 40.
46. Jonathan Edwards, "Religious Affections," *op. cit.*, p. 251; cf. pp. 249, 253.
47. Jonathan Edwards, "Resolutions," "Diary," Faust and Johnson, *op. cit.*, pp. 38, 43f., 46.
48. Smith, *op. cit.*, p. 42.
49. Shorthand notes on the works of Benjamin W. Bacon, *op. cit.*
50. "The Religion of Jesus," *op. cit.*, p. 11.
51. "The Place of the New Testament in the Christian Religion," *op. cit.*, p. 7.
52. "The Place Of The New Testament In The Christian Religion," *op. cit.*, p. 32.
53. Quoted in Delattre, *op. cit.*, p. 205.
54. Jonathan Edwards, "True Grace Distinguished from the Experience of Devils," *op. cit.*, p. 356, had written that Christ's "holiness, or moral excellence" was "that wherein the beauty of the Divine nature does most essentially consist." Commentary in Miller, *op. cit.*, p. 276; Smith, *op. cit.*, p. 35; Delattre, *op. cit.*, pp. 8, 23, 49, 71, 136, 29, 30.
55. Jonathan Edwards, "Excellency of Christ," Faust and Johnson, *op. cit.*, p. 373f.
56. Smith, *op. cit.*, p. 26f.; Delattre, *op. cit.*, p. 183.
57. Miller, *op. cit.*, p. 186.
58. "Toward a Biblical Theology for the Present," *op. cit.*, p. 201.
59. *A Statement of Christian Belief, op. cit.*, p. 10.
60. Comments found in Porter's copy of Rudolf Bultmann's *Jesus and the Word, op. cit.*
61. "On the Spirit," *op. cit.*, p. 3.
62. Cf. Delattre, *op. cit.*, p. 33.
63. "Toward a Biblical Theology for the Present," *op. cit.*, p. 217; comments found in Porter's copy of Rudolf Bultmann's *Jesus and the Word, op. cit.*
64. "Religious Fellowship, Its Basis, Bounds, and Bane," *op. cit.*, p. 20.
65. Comments found in Porter's copy of Rudolf Bultmann's *Jesus and the Word, op. cit.*
66. From an untitled piece on the Old Testament, *op. cit.*, p. 30.
67. *Biblical Theology of the New Testament, op. cit.*, p. 10.
68. "Paul and the Spirit of God," *op. cit.*, p. 45.
69. Jonathan Edwards, "True Grace Distinguished from the Experience of Devils," *op. cit.*, p. 298; cf. Miller, *op. cit.*, p. 325.
70. "Lenten Discussion Club," *op. cit.*

71. "The Place of the Book — The Old Testament in the Religion of Jesus," *op. cit.*, p. 33.
72. *New Testament Theology, op. cit.*, p. 78f.
73. "The Intellectual Value of Theological Training," *op. cit.*, p. 8.
74. "Problems Old and New," *op. cit.*, p. 3.
75. "Historic Fact and Poetic Truth in the Old Testament," *op. cit.*, p. 42.
76. "Our Rights and Duties as to the Bible," *op. cit.*, p. 4.
77. "The Place Of The New Testament In The Christian Religion," *op. cit* , p 53.
78. Jonathan Edwards, "Remarks on the Essays on the Principles of Morality and Natural Religion, In a Letter to a Minister of the Church of Scotland," Faust and Johnson, *op. cit.*, p. 314.
79. Letter to Mr. Chas. Wingate, *op. cit.*
80. "The Spirit of Christianity and the Jesus of History," *op. cit.*, p. 70.
81. Smith, *op. cit.*, p. 7.
82. "What Jesus Christ Means to Me," *op. cit.*, p. 397.
83. "Toward a Biblical Theology for the Present," *op. cit.*, p. 240.
84. Quoted in Delattre, *op. cit.*, p. 154.
85. Cf. *ibid.*, p. 157.
86. Shorthand notes on the works of Benjamin W. Bacon, *op. cit.*
87. Cf. Smith, *op. cit.*, p. 53.
88. "The Religion Of The Spirit," *op. cit.*, p. 12.
89. "The Problem," *op. cit.*, p. 5; Shorthand notes on the works of Benjamin W. Bacon, *op. cit.*
90. "Historical Facts and Religious Values in the Old Testament," *op. cit.*, p. 72.
91. "The Place of Christ in the Christian Religion," *op. cit.*, p. 72.
92. *Ibid., passim*; "The Religion Of The Spirit," *op. cit.*, pp. 23, 36; "On the Spirit," *op. cit., passim*.
93. An untitled fragment on the Fourth Gospel, *op. cit.*, p. 2.
94. *Ibid.*, p. 6.
95. "Interpreters of the Bible and Discoverers of God," *op. cit.*, p. 12.
96. Jonathan Edwards, "Of Being," Faust and Johnson, *op. cit.*, p. 23.
97. *The Mind of Christ in Paul, op. cit.*, p. 88.
98. Jonathan Edwards, "Of Being," *op. cit.*, p. 21.
99. "On the Spirit," *op. cit.*, p. 9.
100. Cf. Miller, *op. cit.*, pp. 63, 292.
101. "The Word of God and the Spirit of God," *op. cit.*, p. 25.
102. Cf. ch. III, n. 2.
103. "Interpreters of the Bible and Discoverers of God," *op. cit.*, p. 11.
104. "On Retiring and Early Years at Yale," unpublished (n.d.).
105. "Historic Fact and Poetic Truth in the Old Testament," *op. cit.*, p. 34; cf. "The Religious and the Historical Uses of the Bible," *op. cit., passim*.
106. *The Mind of Christ in Paul, op. cit.*, pp. 63, 85, 139.
107. Shorthand notes on the works of Benjamin W. Bacon, *op. cit.*

108. "The Place of the Sacred Book in the Christian Religion," *op. cit.*, p. 265.
109. *New Testament Theology, op. cit.*, p. 46.
110. Shorthand notes on the works of Benjamin W. Bacon, *op. cit.*
111. In reference to his old friend Bacon, for whom such talk smacked of legalism, Porter stated that on questions of analysis, composition, sources, authorship and date of the New Testament documents, his friend was free, independent of tradition and often radical, though not infrequently he gave judgments of value and ultimate truth on the side of traditional Christian teaching now rendered problematical. This is the entire burden of Porter's evaluation of his colleague Bacon's work.
112. Of Troeltsch, Porter urged, "read anything of this German you can," "History of Biblical Conceptions: Revelation and Inspiration," *op. cit.*, p. 33.
113. "Toward a Biblical Theology for the Present," *op. cit.*, p. 229.
114. "The Spirit of Christianity and the Jesus of History," *op. cit.*, p. 43.
115. *Biblical Theology of the New Testament, op. cit.*, p. 109.
116. "The Spirit of Christianity and the Jesus of History," *op. cit.*, p. 30.
117. "The Ideals of Seminaries and the Needs of Churches," *op. cit.*, p. 30.
118. *A Statement of Christian Belief, op. cit.*, p. 4.
119. "Historical Facts and Religious Values in the Old Testament," *op. cit.*, p. 28f.
120. "The Spirit of God in the Minds of Men," *op. cit.*, p. 6.
121. Matthew Arnold, *Literature & Dogma, An Essay Towards a Better Apprehension of the Bible* (London: Smith, Elder & Co., 1873), p. 230.
122. Cf. "The Place of Apocalyptical Conceptions in the Thought of Paul," *op. cit.*, p. 186; *New Testament Theology, op. cit.*, p. 142; *The Mind of Christ in Paul, op. cit.*, p. 166; Shorthand notes on the works of Benjamin W. Bacon, *op. cit.*
123. "The Place of Apocalyptical Conceptions in the Thought of Paul," *op. cit.*, p. 185f.; *New Testament Theology, op. cit.*, pp. 74, 142.
124. An untitled piece on the relation of the New Testament to Jesus, *op. cit.*, p. 26.
125. Horace Bushnell, *God in Christ, Three Discourses delivered at New Haven, Cambridge, and Andover, with a Preliminary Dissertation on Language* (Hartford: Brown and Parsons, 1849), pp. 30, 43.
126. *Ibid.*, p. 44.
127. *Ibid.*, p. 79f., 55.
128. *Ibid.*, p. 69f.
129. *Biblical Theology of the New Testament, op. cit.*, p. 83.
130. "Religion of the Spirit," *op. cit.*, p. 34f.
131. "The Place Of The New Testament In The Christian Religion," *op. cit.*, p. 18f.
132. *New Testament Theology, op. cit.*, p. 104; *New Testament Theology: Supplementary Material, op. cit.*, pp. 18-20, 24; Shorthand notes on

the works of Benjamin W. Bacon, *op. cit.*; "The Spirit of Christianity and the Jesus of History," *op. cit.*, p. 30.

133. "Religious Fellowship, Its Basis, Bounds and Bane," *op. cit.*, pp. 19, 28; "Historic Fact and Poetic Truth in the Old Testament," *op. cit.*, pp. 10, 17, 47; "The Place of the New Testament in the Christian Religion," *op. cit.*, p. 10.

134. Jonathan Edwards, "Religious Affections," *op. cit.*, p. 235; cf. Delattre, *op. cit.*, p. 160.

135. Comments found in Porter's copy of Rudolf Bultmann's *Jesus and the Word, op. cit.*

136. Samuel H. Monk, *The Sublime, A Study of Critical Theories in XVIII-Century England* (Ann Arbor: The University of Michigan Press, 1962), pp. 13, 15f., 27, 45, 55, 59, 233.

137. *Ibid.*, pp. 77, 80.

138. "Toward a Biblical Theology for the Present," *op. cit.*, p. 211, and Arnold, *op. cit.*, pp. 83, 190, 200, 214f.

139. Bushnell, *op. cit.*, pp. 60, 74, 77.

140. Cf. Delattre, *op. cit.*, p. 146.

141. Jonathan Edwards, "Religious Affections," *op. cit.*, pp. 229, 247; Jonathan Edwards, "Freedom of the Will," Faust and Johnson, *op. cit.*, pp. 263, 268f.; Miller, *op. cit.*, p. 189; Smith, *op. cit.*, pp. 3, n. 5, 13, 15, 31, 33f.

142. Miller, *op. cit.*, p. 292.

143. Cf. Delattre, *op. cit.*, p. 131.

144. Cf. Smith, *op. cit.*, p. 12.

145. Delattre, *op. cit.*, p. 51.

146. A contrast reflected, e.g., throughout Winslow's Pulitzer Prizewinning biography of Edwards; cf. Ola Elizabeth Winslow, *Jonathan Edwards, 1703-1758* (New York: Collier Books, 1961).

147. Letter to Mr. Chas. Wingate, *op. cit.*; "Revelation, Book of," *A Dictionary of the Bible*, ed. James Hastings (New York: Charles Scribner's Sons, 1901-1904), IV, 265; "The Bearing of Historical Studies on the Religious Use of the Bible," *op. cit.*, p. 260f.; "Toward a Biblical Theology for the Present," *op. cit.*, pp. 217, 219.

148. Bushnell, *op. cit.*, pp. 49, 53.

149. "The Place Of The New Testament In The Christian Religion," *op. cit.*, p. 37.

150. Monk, *op. cit.*, p. 82.

151. Bushnell, *op. cit.*, p. 91.

152. "Things Greater and Less in the Bible," *op. cit.*, pp. 117, 121; "Paul's Belief in Life after Death," *op. cit.*, pp. 239, 249; "Toward a Biblical Theology for the Present," *op. cit.*, p. 227; Shorthand notes on the works of Benjamin W. Bacon, *op. cit.*

153. *New Testament Theology, op. cit.*, p. 101; *Biblical Theology of the New Testament, op. cit.*, p. 102; "Our Rights and Duties as to the Bible," *op. cit.*, p. 4.

154. *The Messages of the Apocalyptical Writers, op. cit.*, p. 280.
155. "The Sayings of Jesus about the First and the Last," *op. cit.*, p. 109f.
156. "The Bearing of Historical Studies on the Religious Use of the Bible," *op. cit.*, p. 256.
157. "The Christian Hope in Times of War," *op. cit.*, p. 50f.; "The Place of Apocalyptical Conceptions in the Thought of Paul," *op. cit.*, p. 185f.; *Biblical Theology of the New Testament, op. cit.*, p. 64; *New Testament Theology, op. cit.*, pp. 74-77; *The Mind of Christ in Paul, op. cit.*, pp. 166, 312.
158. *New Testament Theology, op. cit.*, pp. 34-36.
159. Arnold, *op. cit.*, pp. 93, 105f., 152, 190.
160. "The Liberal and the Ritschlian Theology of Germany," *op. cit.*, p. 449.
161. Miller, *op. cit.*, p. 260.
162. Jonathan Edwards, "Freedom of the Will," *op. cit.*, p. 300.
163. *Ibid.*, pp. 271, 274, 278, 281, 284f., 290, 294f., 300, 303-05; "Remarks on the Essays on the Principles of Morality and Natural Religion," *op. cit.*, pp. 310-12, 314f.
164. "Christian Thinking about Christ," *op. cit.*, p. 8.
165. Cf. Monk, *op. cit.*, pp. 92, 100, 204, 223, 227-31.
166. "Historic Fact and Poetic Truth in the Old Testament," *op. cit.*, p. 14f.
167. *Ibid.*, p. 29; "Toward a Biblical Theology for the Present," *op. cit.*, p. 210.
168. Cf. Ernst von Aster, *Geschichte der Philosophie* (Stuttgart: Alfred Kröner, 1956), 11. Auflage, p. 365f.; Frank Thilly, *A History of Philosophy* (New York: Henry Holt and Company, 1957), Third Edition, pp. 510ff.; W. Windelband, *A History of Philosophy*, trans. James H. Tufts (New York: The Macmillan Company, 1901), pp. 624, 632, 643f., 660, 681; cf. also Emanuel Hirsch, *Geschichte der neueren evangelischen Theologie* (Gütersloh: C. Bertelsmann, 1949-1954), V, 275, 280, 574, 588, and Horst Stephan, *Geschichte der Deutschen Evangelischen Theologie*, 2te neubearbeitete Auflage von M. Schmidt (Berlin: Alfred Töpelmann, 1960), pp. 126, 128, 207, 217, 219, 298.
169. "The Word of God and the Spirit of God," *op. cit.*, pp. 23-25.
170. *A Statement of Christian Belief, op. cit.*, p. 4.
171. Arnold, *op. cit.*, p. 156; cf. *Biblical Theology of the New Testament, op. cit.*, p. 62.
172. Bushnell, *op. cit.*, p. 75.
173. Shorthand notes on the works of Benjamin W. Bacon, *op. cit.*
174. Jonathan Edwards, "Of Being," *op. cit.*, p. 19; "The Excellency of Christ," *op. cit.*, p. 121; "Freedom of the Will," *op. cit.*, p. 289; "Religious Affections," *op. cit.*, 254.
175. Letter from Shirley Jackson Case, December 18, 1914.
176. "Religious Fellowship, Its Basis, Bounds, and Bane," *op. cit.*, pp. 21ff.
177. "The Place Of The New Testament In The Christian Religion," *op. cit.*, p. 92.

178. "Paul and the Spirit of God," *op. cit.*, p. 43, n. 4.

179. "Toward a Biblical Theology for the Present," *op. cit.*, p. 225.

180. William Wordsworth, "Tintern Abbey," *The Standard Book of British and American Verse* (New York: The Garden City Publishing Co., Inc., 1932), p. 258.

181. Bushnell, *op. cit.*, p. 96.

182. Arnold, *op. cit.*, p. 233.

183. Quoted in Delattre, *op. cit.*, p. 56.

184. *New Testament Theology, op. cit.*, p. 119.

185. *The Mind of Christ in Paul, op. cit.*, p. 304.

186. *Ibid.*

187. *New Testament Theology, op. cit.*, p. 104.

188. "The Christian Hope in Times of War," *op. cit.*, p. 37.

189. "On the Spirit," *op. cit.*, p. 4.

190. George Santayana, *Character and Opinion in the United States* (New York: W. W. Norton & Co., 1967), p. 213.

191. Reinhold Niebuhr, *Does Civilization Need Religion?* (New York: The Macmillan Co., 1928), pp. 46, 216.

192. *Ibid.*, p. 80.

193. *Ibid.*, p. 236.

194. *Ibid.*, p. 198.

195. Reinhold Niebuhr, *Leaves from the Notebook of a Tamed Cynic* (Chicago: Willett, Clark & Colby, 1929), pp. 33, 51, 56, 121.

196. *Ibid.*, p. 33.

197. Niebuhr, *Does Civilization Need Religion? op. cit.*, p. 31.

198. *Ibid.*, p. 216.

199. Niebuhr, *Leaves from the Notebook of a Tamed Cynic, op. cit.*, p. 157.

200. Quoted in *ibid.*, p. 73.

201. Reinhold Niebuhr, "Intellectual Autobiography," *Reinhold Niebuhr, His Religious, Social, and Political Thought*, ed. Charles W. Kegley and Robert W. Bretall (New York: The Macmillan Company, 1956), p. 4.

202. Niebuhr, *Does Civilization Need Religion? op. cit.*, pp. 3, 161, 205.

203. *Ibid.*, p. 64; cf. pp. 68, 167.

204. *Ibid.*, pp. 69, 101.

205. *Ibid.*, pp. 161, 234.

206. *Ibid.*, pp. 196, 205.

207. *Ibid.*, p. 213.

208. *Ibid.*, pp. 9, 200, 218.

209. Niebuhr, *Leaves from the Notebook of a Tamed Cynic, op. cit.*, p. 90.

210. *Ibid.*, p. 85.

211. Reinhold Niebuhr, "Ten Years That Shook My World," *The Christian Century*, LVI, 17 (April 26, 1939), p. 545.

212. Hermann Hesse, *Das Glasperlenspiel*, Versuch einer Lebensbeschreibung des Magisters Ludi Josef Knecht samt Knechts hinterlassenen Schriften (Hamburg: Fischer Bücherei, 1967), p. 132. Author's translation.

213. By 1900, Porter had written fifteen pieces, including several articles in James Hastings' *A Dictionary of the Bible*, though a 1934 University of Chicago doctoral dissertation dealing with the history of the interpretation and criticism of the New Testament in this country from 1620-1900 made no mention of him. Benjamin Bacon had published more than forty essays by that time, though the dissertation's bibliography refers to only one. Had the candidate consulted Shirley Jackson Case, Bacon and Porter's old pupil? Cf. Donald Stanley Klaiss, *The History of the Interpretation and Criticism of the New Testament in America, 1620-1900* (unpublished Ph.D. dissertation, Divinity School, University of Chicago, 1934). In Paul Feine's *Theologie des Neuen Testaments* (Berlin: Evangelische Verlagsanstalt, 1950), pp. 164 and 449, there are two brief references to "Fr Chr Porter."

A PORTER BIBLIOGRAPHY
Listing Titles Not Included in the Footnotes

"The Moon by Jupiter!" *The Courant*, March 16, 1885.

"The Afternoon Tea," A Ballad of June, *The Evening Post*, June 23, 1885.

"Postal Card Grammar," To the Editor of *The Courant*, September 15, 1885.

Review of *Messianic Prophecy: The Prediction of the Fulfillment of Redemption Through the Messiah*, by C. A. Briggs, *The New Englander and Yale Review*, XLVI, 1887.

"The Spirits in Prison — A Neglected Theory Reconsidered," *The New Englander and Yale Review*, XIII, August, 1888.

"Philo, and His Latest Interpreter," *The New Englander*, XIV, February, 1889.

"The Jewish Literature of New Testament Times: How Should It Be Studied?" *The Old and New Testament Student*, IX, No. 3, September, 1889.

"The Religious Ideas of the Book of Ecclesiasticus I," *The Old and New Testament Student*, XIII, No. 1, July, 1891.

"The Religious Ideas of the Book of Ecclesiasticus II," *The Old and New Testament Student*, XIII, No. 2, August, 1891.

"The Gospel of John as a Book for Its Time," *The Sunday School Times*, December 12, 1891.

"The Religious Ideas of the First Book of Maccabees," *The Old and New Testament Student*, XIV, No. 2, February, 1892.

"The Psalms of the Pharisees," *The Biblical World*, IV, No. 3, September, 1894.

"The Apocrypha," *The Biblical World*, VIII, No. 4, October, 1896.

"Apocrypha," "Canopy," "Judith," "Book of Judith," "Prayer of Manasses," "Proselyte," *Dictionary of the Bible*, ed. James Hastings, Vols. I-IV, New York: Charles Scribner's Sons, 1901-1904.

91

Review of *Einleitung in Das Neue Testament*, Band I by Theodor Zahn, *The American Journal of Theology*, II, No. 3, July, 1898.

"The Yecer Hara: A Study in the Jewish Doctrine of Sin," *Biblical and Semitic Studies*, Yale Bi-centennial Publications, New York: Charles Scribner's Sons, 1901.

Review of *The Historical New Testament* by James Moffatt, *The Congregationalist and Christian World*, July 6, 1901.

Review of *The Messianic Hope in the New Testament* by Shailer Mathews, *The American Journal of Theology*, 1905.

"George B. Stevens," *Yale Divinity Quarterly*, III, 1906.

"The Joys of Great Books," "False and True Paths to Joy," *A Year of Good Cheer*, by Delia Lyman Porter, Boston: 1906.

"The Imitation of Christ," *The Homiletic Review*, LII, July-December, 1906.

"The Pre-existence of the Soul in the Book of Wisdom and in the Rabbinical Writings," *The American Journal of Theology*, XII, No. 1, January, 1908.

"The Gospel of John as a Book for the Future," *The Sunday School Times*, December 26, 1911.

"Lewis Orsmond Brastow, D.D." A Memorial Address given in Marquand Chapel, January 9, 1913, *Yale Divinity Quarterly*, IX, January, 1913.

Review of *Jesus in the Nineteenth Century and After* by Heinrich Weinel, *Yale Divinity Quarterly*, March, 1914.

Review of *The Book of Job Interpreted* by James Strahan, *Yale Divinity Quarterly*, March, 1914.

Review of *He Opened to Us the Scriptures* by Benjamin W. Bacon, *Yale Divinity Quarterly*, 1923.

Review of *The Apostolic Message* by Benjamin W. Bacon, *Yale Divinity Quarterly*, 1923.

"Professor Bacon's Retirement," *Yale Divinity News*, March, 1928.

     1928.

"Does Paul Claim to have Known the Historical Jesus?" *Journal of Biblical Literature*, XLVII, 1928.

"Light From Paul on Present Problems of Christian Thinking," *Yale Divinity News*, May, 1929.

The obituary of Benjamin W. Bacon, *New Haven Journal-Courier*, February 4, 1932.